W9-AWS-284

Arks for Learning

Arks for Learning

A short history of Oxford library buildings

by

Giles Barber

OXFORD

The Oxford Bibliographical Society

1995

ISBN 0 901420 51 4

A Catalogue record for this book is
available from the British Library

Contents

COVER   Corpus Christi College. Building early sixteenth century, stalls c.1604, wooden ceiling 1843. The stalls originally had only two shelves above the sloping desks but a further two were added c.1700, the join being masked by beading just visible above the framed catalogue Tables at the ends of the stalls. Equally the desks at first had a chain gap between them and the shelves when the desks were fixed down to their supports. Later, possibly when shelves were added below, the chain gap was filled in and the desks were hinged to this wood, first with long bracket hinges, later with small ones. The hinged desk can be held upright by means of a hook on the vertical ends of the stalls. Corpus has kept much of its ironwork for chaining and locking the books, some of which can just be seen at the end of the stall on the left. Unusually the library has been retained for the current use of the college, the majority of the older books having been housed elsewhere and modern ones put in their place. Cushions, modern lighting and a foot-rest bar have also been installed, thus encouraging the continued use of this historic room.

FRONTISPIECE   Duke Humfrey's Library, close-up of shelved volumes. One chained volume is shown open on the reading desk. The chain was fixed to the fore-edge of the upper cover of the book. Such volumes would have to be shelved fore-edge out as shown by the upper books which have the numbers on the fore-edge. The volumes were turned round about 1800 when the white paint, and later gilt, lettering was added. The metalwork on the crosspiece of the shelves is original but the chain gap, between the reading desk and the shelf, has been filled in.

Preface

As Giles Barber points out in this most interesting study, Oxford holds a large part of the national written and printed heritage in its various libraries, many of which, architecturally, are themselves part of that heritage. Historically, Oxford's local building materials (for the most part limestone and wood) and the somewhat moist and cool atmospheric conditions of the Thames Valley, have been very friendly to the parchment and papers of which books and manuscripts are made and have played their part in ensuring the survival of so many. Yet while the collections themselves have fulfilled their purpose in attracting the attention of many scholars, no-one has in recent years undertaken any historical survey of the buildings and furniture constructed to house them. The study presented here makes absorbing reading, charting as it does a series of responses over time to the changing demands placed upon library materials as the pursuit of knowledge through books (now more fashionably called 'research'), previously the preserve of the few, is now undertaken by so many.

Buildings and furniture from the later middle ages onwards survive in Oxford to demonstrate how many of the country's greatest architects and many lesser-known (often unknown) makers of furniture have applied themselves to designing settings worthy of the books. In the last century and a half the needs of the reader have perhaps come to predominate over the needs of the materials that they have come to read, with results that are not always happy.

Altogether it is a fascinating story the evidence for which is all around us in Oxford. Giles Barber has performed an important service in gathering much of this evidence together between one set of covers. The notion of a library as an ark saving learning from the deluge of ignorance was applied by Francis Bacon to the Bodleian, but it might have been applied to many other library buildings in Oxford. Their history is admirably set forth here.

David Vaisey
Bodley's Librarian

Acknowledgements

Any work which attempts to touch on the buildings and history of so many institutions offers hostages to fortune: the use of the numerous books and articles on these aspects of Oxford has helped the author along his way but he could not have managed without the kindness, help and advice of a whole host of friends. To the Council of the Oxford Bibliographical Society I am grateful for accepting yet another book, to the Society's General Editors, Dr H. Woudhuysen and Mr J. McLaverty, I owe much for their editorial expertise, while my warmest thanks go to Bodley's Librarian for his interest and advice, as well as for his preface. All those interested in the history of Oxford libraries have, for several decades, learned to rely on the knowledge and kindness of Paul Morgan. Countless college librarians have allowed me to visit their libraries and have answered questions – I am grateful to them all. Numerous others have read the text in part or whole, corrected errors and contributed much: hoping to omit no one I would mention particularly William and Madeleine Barber, Robert Beddard, Alan Bell, Penelope Bulloch, William Clennell, Howard Colvin, David Cooper, Nicholas Cronk, Joanna Dodsworth, Michael Dudley, Polly Friedhoff, Malcolm Graham, Anne Hamerton, Brian Harrison, Roger Highfield, Anthony Hobson, Diane Kay, Julian Roberts, John Simmons, David Sturdy, and Michael Turner. Most importantly it will be clear that this book could not present its subject in this manner without the skill of Mr J.W. Thomas, who has photographed historic Oxford for so long that his magnificent photographs are not only illustrations but themselves both history and legend. This selection is but a sample on one specific subject from his wide archive. For their help and encouragement I offer all the above my warmest thanks – all errors remain, as usual, the responsibility of the author.

Giles Barber
The Taylor Institution

List of illustrations

The dates given are those of construction or reorganisation. All photographs or reproductions are modern unless their date is shown in parentheses.

BACK COVER   Double doors in the 1934 extension to the Radcliffe Science Library, carved in wood by Eric Gill (1882–1940), and representing famous scientists associated with Oxford. The initials of each person feature in their panel, the latter running in chronological order, from top left across and then down both doors.

a) Roger Bacon (c.1220–92). A Franciscan philosopher, he was educated at Oxford and worked both there and at Paris on optics, alchemy and astrology. Known as the 'Doctor Mirabilis', he was one of the founders of modern experimental science and foresaw the magnifying properties of convex lenses.

b) William Harvey (1578–1657). Cambridge educated, he was physician to both James I and Charles I, and the discoverer of the circulation of the blood (1628). Coming, like other scientists, to Oxford during the Civil War (a move which led to the foundation of the Royal Society), he became Warden of Merton College in 1645.

c) Robert Boyle (1627–91). An Irish-born physicist and chemist working in his own laboratory in University College from 1659, he conducted experimental work on air, vacuum and respiration, propounding Boyle's law, by which the pressure and volume of gas are inversely proportionate.

d) Sir Christopher Wren (1632–1723). Educated at Wadham College, he was appointed professor of astronomy in 1661, soon branching out into architecture. He designed the Sheldonian in 1663, and, following the Great Fire, many City churches including St. Paul's.

e) Robert Hook (1635–1703). A chemist and physicist educated at Christ Church, he became Secretary of the Royal Society in 1677. His experiments on the chemical basis of respiration followed those of Boyle, while his studies on elasticity led to the balance spring for watches. He was also responsible for developments in the telescope and microscope, and anticipated Newton with the law of inverse squares.

f) John James Dillenius (1687–1747). German-born, Dillenius became the first Sherardian professor of botany. He welcomed Linnaeus on his visit to Oxford, started the important herbarium there, and was responsible for the introduction of Oxford ragwort to the United Kingdom.

All original photographs are by J. W. Thomas except the following, kindly provided as follows: The Ashmolean Museum no 36; Balliol College no 42; G. Barber no 54; the Bodleian nos 4,7,8,9,20,26,29,43,46; M. Dudley nos 2,48,49; N. McBeath no 71; the Oxford Union Society no 47; the Oxfordshire County Council nos 52,53; J. Slatter no 70; the Archivist, St Edmund Hall nos 30,55.

Arks for Learning:

A SHORT HISTORY OF OXFORD LIBRARY BUILDINGS

Introduction

The Bodleian is undoubtedly Oxford's most famous library. From the outside at least its historic buildings are as well known to the tourists as the books and manuscripts inside are to the scholars who come, as do the tourists, from all over the world. It houses however only just over half the total stock held by the University and the colleges of Oxford (today over nine million volumes), and the latter in particular have not only famous and ancient collections but also library buildings of both beauty and historic interest. The aim of the present publication is to document how Oxford's library collections have been housed over the ages and to illustrate this from the many surviving features which can still be seen in various buildings today. To understand how study and storage systems have evolved will assist a comprehension of a rich but complex information resource, encourage a better appreciation of this great heritage, and allow the very considerable problems which its conservation raises to be seen in their historical context. The long timespan of Oxford's libraries, like that of its other buildings and its gardens, presents a living museum where those fortunate enough to frequent these places, even for a short time, can see and understand something of the way in which, over the years, forces, intellectual, artistic, technical and financial have interacted to mould the setting, workplaces and learned materials of a great university.

The Medieval Period

Very little is known about library buildings in classical Greece or Rome but the Roman architect Vitruvius, writing in about 40 BC, says 'There is another advantage which must be taken of the site, that is to ensure that rooms for sleeping in, and libraries, must always face the rising sun. Bathrooms and winter apartments should face the winter sun; rooms with paintings and other curiosities, which require an even light, to the north...' and he later explains this further by saying, 'Bedrooms and libraries must face the rising sun because their function requires the morning light and moreover because the books come to less harm in such libraries than in those facing the south and west which are more subject to worms and damp since the humidity caused by the winds feeds the worms and rots the books'. These environmental principles were sound and their spirit motivated the architects of Oxford libraries from the Middle Ages even until recent times.

The first recorded reference to Oxford as a town dates back to the year 912, and it seems that a small township may have grown up around the monastery founded by St. Frideswide in the eighth century, probably on the site of the present cathedral. Oxford thrived and, under royal patronage, was one of the largest towns in England by the early eleventh century. The Normans settled and built the castle, following which came more peaceful times and the growth of suburbs both within and outside the city walls. The University established itself in Oxford during the twelfth century, probably because of the existence in the city of various religious houses and through their protection by the king. In the late thirteenth and fourteenth centuries the Benedictine monasteries, aiming to revive monastic learning, set up a number of communities and, while many of these were later dissolved in the sixteenth century because of their monastic nature, others provided the foundation for the new secular colleges. The town meanwhile suffered severely through economic depression, and with the Black Death the population declined during the fourteenth and fifteenth centuries so that even land inside the walls became cheap, and colleges such as New College and All Souls were able to buy property in the very centre of the city.

In the early medieval period manuscripts were produced in the scriptoria of the monasteries, each being the result of slow and careful work. In the twelfth century manuscripts, often the Bible or the works of the Fathers of the Church, were commonly folio in format, written in large, legible hands on parchment and bound in stout leather over wooden boards, frequently decorated with a quincunx of five large-headed nails. The latter protected the volume from wear while it rested on the wide, sloping desks usual at those times or on the lectern in the choir. The thirteenth-century movement away from the monasteries and towards the new university centres changed the whole nature of demand and therefore of production. Students from many different regions congregated in university towns and created a need for more and more books on the subjects dealt with in the scholastic curriculum. The rapid production of portable and inexpensive, undecorated, texts introduced an almost industrial concept into bookmaking. The process shifted therefore largely to the universities where books became smaller in format, the number of leaves in each gathering increased, a layout with two columns on each page became regular, ornamentation was abandoned, and the contraction of words was in frequent use. Copies were made by scribes working for stationers who divided out the gatherings of the master copy of a text among them so that each part could be reproduced simultaneously. This *pecia* system became generalized in the thirteenth century. Trade regulations aimed at providing students with accurate and cheap texts.

Throughout the Middle Ages manuscript books were normally read, as they were written, at desks set around monastery cloisters and they were either kept there or in wooden-lined cupboards around the walls nearby. Within the cupboards they were shelved flat, and the use of this kind of storage had been regular practice right back to Roman times when rolls were similarly housed in *armaria*. Numerous paintings and manuscript illuminations depict such cupboards. In the later Middle Ages books were also kept in chests which were particularly convenient for those, such as rich clerics, who travelled around the country. Many volumes of the twelfth and early thirteenth centuries have a half-moon shaped ear or lug of leather protruding at each end beyond the spine and it may well be that these were to assist in pulling the volume out of such chests. With the rise of university, as opposed to monastic, reading, books were increasingly borrowed and taken away to be studied or copied. When members of the University were in need of a financial loan, to return to some distant home or for other reasons, they could pledge a valuable volume and the pledge, like other university moneys, would be placed in the University Chest, which was the strong room for such items from the mid-thirteenth century. The University's finance department is indeed still called 'The University Chest' but of the older chests used in this manner only a few survive. The oldest is the Chest of the Five Keys, recorded in 1427 (and now exhibited in the Ashmolean Museum), while the lighter, painted, version of 1668 is in the office of the Secretary of the Chest (the head financial officer). Such chests often had several keys and different keyholders for greater security. There are also some surviving examples of fourteenth-century wooden, general-purpose chests: one in Merton College library (where library chests were given up in about 1377), a French one at New College, and a late sixteenth-century metal-bound chest, decorated with coats of arms and having a complex locking system, which belonged to Sir Thomas Bodley and which is now kept in the Bodleian Library for the receipt of donations.

[1]

The University Church of St Mary the Virgin may be on the site of a late ninth- or early tenth-century church situated near what was then the east gate of the city and away from the bustle of the city centre at Carfax. It was for this reason, perhaps, the focus of the early university. A 'school' or lecture room was located here in 1190 and by the thirteenth century parchment-makers, scribes, illuminators and bookbinders were to be found nearby in Catte Street, on the site of what is now the Radcliffe Camera. About 1320 the Old Congregation House was built onto the east side of St Mary's tower with money given by Thomas Cobham, Bishop of Worcester, who intended the room above to house the books he was going to give to the University. However he died in 1327 before the work was complete. His executors pawned the books to pay the funeral costs and other debts but they were redeemed and deposited in Oriel College (the 'House of the Blessed Mary the Virgin'). Shortly after 1337 the University declared them to be their property and carried them off to the room in St Mary's church. In 1367 a University statute decreed that the books should be chained but the full installation of the library in the upper room, then complete with glazed windows, was not achieved before 1410. The 1367 statute also allowed for the sale of certain volumes in order to establish a post for a chaplain who would both pray for the soul of Thomas Cobham and look after the books. This was therefore the first appointment of a University Librarian and marks the real establishment of the first University Library, a building which served until the construction of Duke Humfrey's Library, and which, structurally, can still be seen today.

[2]

The pattern established in the planning of Bishop Cobham's library was to act as a model for a number of college libraries built shortly after. It is the earliest example of a first-floor library, the usual location from then onwards until the late nineteenth century. The room was sixty-three feet long and nineteen feet wide, orientated here on an east/west axis. It was lit on either side by seven tall and narrow single-light windows, with a triple-lit larger west window. Traces of these windows remain only on the south side, those on the north having been widened and remodelled. There were originally eight bays for double-sided lecterns, each six feet long and standing at right angles to the wall spaces between the windows, the intervening readers' benches being aligned on the windows themselves. The lectern stands reached a height of five feet seven inches at the apex of their sharply sloping sides and thus required their readers to look up rather than down at the books they were reading. Merton College is known to have had books from as early as 1264 and the library was in use before the full establishment of Bishop Cobham's, but it adopted the same basic organisation either from the latter or possibly from elsewhere since it is known that the Warden and his mason went to London to see the library of the Preaching Friars. The Merton library, the most important early library still in use in Oxford, was constructed on the first floor of Mob Quad, the northern part of which dates from the early fourteenth century and the southern from 1371-78. It spreads in an L-shape on to two sides of the first floor of the quadrangle (being therefore on two axes, north/south and east/west) and was clearly intended to cater for a substantial number of books, the number by 1375 having been put as high as 500. The windows and the window bays are smaller than Bishop Cobham's and there is only one entrance staircase, which initially came up at the northern end of the two wings.

[3]

The old library at New College, dating from 1380-86, was also an integral part of the construction of a quadrangle, and similarly on the first floor, but this time on a north/south axis. As at Merton the room is twenty-one feet long but has slightly larger windows (which made for greater bay width and comfort), possibly because there are no end windows. The Exeter College library (no longer extant) in 1383 was smaller, with one main window, and was free standing. The original All Souls library was built in 1440 on a north/south axis in the front quadrangle. It is said to have had fourteen double-sided and four single-sided desks which are calculated as having held up to five hundred manuscripts chained on the sloping reading surfaces or on the shelf below.

At this period college libraries held two kinds of stock: the most frequently needed texts were confined to the library both for security and for general reading; the room where they were kept was called the 'libraria' from the late fourteenth century and the 'bibliotheca' from the sixteenth. The books, mostly of larger size and bound in leather over wooden boards, often with clasps and metal bosses on the covers, had a staple fixed to the middle of the lower edge of one of the covers of the binding. This held a chain connected to a rod running the length of the desk (usually along the lower edge). The volumes were kept flat and in order on the lectern-type stand. Colleges had however many other manuscripts, this second stock being for reading in the Fellows' rooms. [Chaucer, writing in the late 1380s, says that his clerk of Oxford was not 'so worldly for to have office./ For hym was levere have at his beddes heed/ Twenty bookes, clad in blak or reed,/ Of Aristotle and his philosophie,/ Than robes rich, or fithele, or gay sautrie.'] Such secondary stock was distributed among the fellowship in

4

annual 'electiones'. An early All Souls list talks of some 204 'catenati' (or chained) books and 164 'distribuendi'. Later a rich college such as Merton could distribute some 375 books in this way and in 1519 five Fellows received around forty books each in this manner. The practice of chaining library books is first recorded at the Sorbonne (University of Paris) in 1290.

These early libraries usually had a tiled central floor and shutters for the windows, traces of which have been found in the rebates. Glazing for the windows came in early in the fifteenth century but remained imperfect and the cold may have been what prompted Merton to close-board its ceiling for greater warmth in 1502. In view of the draughts early library statutes made much of the need not to leave books open and to ensure that the shutters and windows were closed on leaving. There was no question of heating or of artificial light. Vitruvius's principles of orientation were evidently still relevant. The position and the size of college libraries were of course also subject to the general college building plans. The Magdalen library (1479-83) was wide, being over the cloisters, while that of Corpus Christi College (built in the 1510s) in the south range of the front quad, opposite the gatehouse and equally on the first floor, was integrated into the general design, having smaller, taller (and therefore darker) windows but wider bays.

Numerous gifts and benefactions accrued to the University in the fifteenth century. One of the main donors was Humfrey, Duke of Gloucester (1391-1447), who had fought with his brother, Henry V, in the Hundred Years War and at Agincourt but was also a great bibliophile. His benefactions started in 1411, and in 1439 he gave no fewer than 129 volumes, his gifts probably totalling over 600 in all. The University was then engaged in building a new and ambitious lecture room for theological debate, the Divinity School, and, possibly influenced by the example of Winchester College, it was suggested to the Duke that he might care to fund a library room above, which would be named after him. The Duke approved but, since he died not long after, no funds actually reached the University. The construction of the Divinity School, which had been started in 1420, stagnated for a while and was only completed, thanks largely to the generosity of Thomas Kempe, Bishop of London, in the 1480s. There had however been two major changes of plan: the addition of not only a large library room above but also the insertion into the Schools of a fine vaulted ceiling, contemporary with that at St George's Chapel, Windsor. This addition had made it necessary for the library floor to be raised and the windows to be made higher. The extra weight also required the addition of pinnacles to the buttresses in order to counteract the thrust of the vault. This upper room also required the building of staircases which were housed in two stone turrets at the western end and linked, at ground level, by a porch. The turrets were eventually taken down in the 1630s but can be glimpsed on the Bereblock drawing (which is the basis of the modern logo of the Bodleian) and, for details of the staircase, on the engraved scene at the foot of Bodley's memorial in Merton College chapel. On completion the University's manuscripts were transferred to this new library room from St Mary's, where the old library was left empty. This new room drew its proportions from those of the Divinity School below it, but may also have been influenced by New College library in its spaciousness although, unlike the college, it also had two large and light mullioned end-windows. The reading desks were wide and eight feet long. Although they were later removed, their exact profile is known, having been found shadowed against the wall during restorations in the 1960s. This shows that these double-sided lecterns were approximately 6 feet high, one foot eight inches wide and that the reading surface, starting at a height of four feet three inches, was at an angle of 67 degrees. They were thus true, high, lecterns at which the reader stood to read.

[4,5,6,7]

The sixteenth century was by contrast to see slow development, disastrous losses and, later, very major changes in Oxford library provision, some due to technical innovations, some stemming from new movements in the history of ideas. The basic material of the medieval book was parchment, an animal product but one liable to cockling and therefore often given a firm binding between stiff, wooden boards, held together by clasps in order to keep the textblock flat and firm. The use of paper is said to be first recorded in England in an archive entry at Merton College where its purchase 'for making a register' is mentioned in 1310. Although the production of hand-made paper was a slow process the material nevertheless had great industrial advantages over parchment and was a notable factor in the spread of printing. England had to rely on imported paper until the seventeenth century and locally it was not until the 1680s that the papermills at Wolvercote, near Oxford, started production. The introduction of paper into book production did however have the effect of providing a good supply of a suitable surface for printing, of reducing the weight of books, of easing the use of smaller formats and of allowing for lighter forms of binding. The problems associated with the use of parchment, and therefore with thick wooden boards, meant that the lectern was the natural habitat of such books. In library terms the change to paper resulted not only in more books being produced but also in the fact that the new form of the book was slimmer and lighter and could therefore be shelved more easily and more economically on the vertical rather than on a sloping desk or, horizontally, on the shelf beneath.

When the University had petitioned Duke Humfrey for help in 1444 they instanced in particular the overcrowded nature of Bishop Cobham's library, where so many books were chained to the lecterns that readers got in each other's way: 'Should any student be poring over a single volume, as often happens, he keeps three or four others away on account of the books being chained so closely together.' This testimony also explains why colleges which had not, on foundation, built libraries did so in the middle of the fifteenth century: University College, founded in 1280, in 1440; Balliol College, founded in 1282, in 1431; and Oriel College, founded in 1324, in 1444. Further pressures were about to be added to these problems. In the mid-fifteenth century a number of elements had come together to satisfy the new demand for books. Johann Gensfleisch zum Gutenberg (1394/99-1468) invented both the system of movable types and an ink suitable to go with them. He was therefore able to produce the famous 42-line Bible in Mainz between 1452 and 1456. The effects of this innovation have been considerable but, in local Oxford library terms, they were fairly slow in coming, printing beginning here in 1478 and then occurring only spasmodically for a while.

The Renaissance

Fed early on by gifts from bibliophiles and scholars, the college libraries continued to grow and in the early sixteenth century even started some systematic acquisitions on their own, but these died down towards the 1530s. More drastic was the effect of Henry VIII's Dissolution of the Monasteries (1536), which depleted the monastic foundations, some of which managed nevertheless to re-emerge as secular colleges. The visit of Edward VI's Commissioners in 1550 also wreaked havoc, despoiling much of the University library. Anthony Wood, writing in 1674, records that 'some of those books so taken out by the Reformers were burnt, some sold away for Robin Hoods pennyworths, either to Booksellers, or to Glovers to press their gloves, or Taylors to make measures, or to Bookbinders to cover books bound by them, and some also kept by the Reformers for their own use'. As a result the University in 1556 appointed a committee charged with the sale of the empty shelving from Duke Humfrey's Library, which, in Sir Thomas Bodley's later words, became 'a great desolate room'. Thus numerous works of scholastic philosophy were removed from college libraries, marking a shift away from this traditional study, while at the same time few Protestant books were to be found in the University library when Elizabeth I came to the throne in 1558.

Changes were slowly being made and in many ways a newly founded college such as Corpus Christi symbolised the Renaissance. Corpus, a college established by Bishop Richard Foxe and built in about 1516, was an essentially Humanist body. Its members were allowed to speak either Latin or the recently learnt Greek at meal times and Erasmus, a friend of the founder and his circle, praised what he heard of the library. In the beginning this gave equal place to both manuscripts and printed books. From an organisational point of view however the library remained traditional: the statutes recognising the existence of both a library of chained books, important in form and contents, and a lending collection. The former were still chained from the centre of the lower edge of the binding and, in all probability, initially kept on the lectern system. Colleges founded later, such as St John's and Trinity (both 1555), had the advantage of taking over the sites of former monastic bodies (St Bernard's and Durham Colleges respectively) and, at least in the latter case, had only to do minor repairs to an already existing structure. Similarly Christ Church was able to purchase the lectern stands thrown out of Duke Humfrey's Library and to place them in the refectory of St Frideswide's Priory (1562).

The later sixteenth century saw the beginning of some notable changes in the University as indeed in the nation. This was the age in which the mass of earlier colleges, hitherto largely reserved for graduates, and the lesser residential halls for undergraduates merged to produce the more definitive form of what has been called the 'collegiate university'. Higher education began to attract the Elizabethan and Jacobean governing class, something which, in turn, required the University to evolve some form of responsible organisation and to adhere to orthodoxy. The syllabus remained traditional - if more Protestant - but matriculation by a recognised college became necessary from 1565 and subscription to the Thirty-nine Articles of the Church of England a requirement from 1581. The social composition of the University was both widened and raised, a change which brought about improvements in accommodation, and other similar general developments in colleges which, *inter alia*, led to better libraries.

[8, 9]

Little important building went on however until the 1580s and the major developments taking place then seem to have been the work of two men in particular: Henry Savile, Warden of Merton College, and his friend the diplomat and scholar, Sir Thomas Bodley (1550-1613). Savile became Warden on 1 August 1583 and turned his attention at once to the library, inaugurating new rules on 16 August. The college was also confronted with the bequest of some two hundred books, left by a former Fellow, James Leech, who died in the same month. Moreover many of the books of this period, the works of the Fathers of the Church and the like, were often folio in format. The need for a new solution to the storage problem was urgent. Colleges were not in a position to build new and structurally different libraries and the answer lay therefore in altering the internal arrangement so as to give greater capacity. This new 'stall' system, an evolutionary one still based on the need to chain books, became characteristic of seventeenth-century Oxford. It replaced the traditional lectern, which relied on placing books on single, sloping, reading desks, with a new one consisting of several flat horizontal shelves, tiered one above the other, but with a separate, projecting, reading desk. This system was introduced into the west library at Merton in 1589-90. There the medieval lecterns were replaced by double-sided vertical bookcases, similarly extending in pairs between each window bay and with a fixed double-sided bench between. The reader sat on this bench, an innovation, and looked down (rather than up as with the lectern) at his book which was placed on a desk cantilevered forward at a convenient height. The volume, stored upright on a shelf above and with its fore-edge facing outwards, was secured by the customary chain affixed to one of the vertical front edges of the binding and, at the other end, to a metal bar running the length of the shelf. This allowed the book to be lowered onto the desk. Originally there were only two shelves, one at desk level and another above it, but further shelves were added, first one above and, later, others below. The desk, at which the reader sat looking down at his book, was at a noticeably shallower slope than that of the lectern. It was fixed to supporting beams running across the case and had a three-inch gap in front of the shelf so that the book-chains could hang down and be fixed to the iron retaining bar below. The bars for the chains were locked into the uprights of the cases. Much of all this can still be seen at Merton today although the later additional shelves now complicate an understanding of the simple nature of the original system and all the original chains have been removed. In fact only two books at Oxford remain chained in the genuine manner (one in Duke Humfrey's Library and one in Merton) but the Wells and Hereford cathedral libraries (although the latter has been dismounted, stored and remounted later) still present the full picture of a chained library on the seventeenth-century 'stall' system. At Cambridge the medieval library equally suffered dispersal but, the restoration of the library coming later in the sixteenth century than at Oxford, the books were, in general, not chained.

[10, 11]

As we see them today virtually all the early stalls (except those at Merton) have hinged desks but it is most likely that this represents a later evolutionary stage of their history. To go by the evidence at Merton and at Corpus, the early stall with only two or three shelves had a chain-bar through the upright ends under the desk-level shelf (from which the chain rose through the chain-gap between the desk and the bottom shelf to the volume resting on it) and two other chain-bars, one in front of each of the upper shelves. Chains, long enough to allow their volume to be lowered down to the desk, hung down in front of the shelved volumes. As further storage was required (probably in the eighteenth century) shelves were added under the desk level; access to this area then became necessary, thus requiring the desk to be raised. These books below the desk were not chained. At this point the desks, which had hitherto been fixed to their supports (probably by wooden pins or dowels), were cut free from them and were hinged back against the uprights of the stall with fairly large-armed hinges, one being placed at each end. At some later stage still, possibly after the removal of chains, the chain-gap was filled in by a long piece of wood to which the desks were then fixed, along the inner join, with a less visible hinge. A special metal clip on the uprights at the ends allowed the desk to be held in a raised position. At first the whole desk was lifted as one but later desks were cut so that there was one section to each tier or press.

The new presses (as the stall shelving was called) were taller than the lecterns and consequently darkened the room so that at Merton large dormer windows had to be added on the (east-facing) quad side and the library's internal arrangement altered in 1606 by moving the staircase to the central junction of the two wings. The east library too was reshelved in 1623 and dormer windows similarly added on the north side. The subject layout is also worth noting: theology, law and medicine were kept in the east library and arts (the last in this official order of the faculties) in the west one. The choicest items were kept protected in cupboards either on the spacious central landing or in the first bays to the north. Theology, the 'Queen of the sciences' and the most studied, was the best provided for and may have been given the well-lit, south-facing, side. The same system subsists in Duke Humfrey's Library.

[12, 13]

The new fashion caught on fast and by 1600 similar stall shelving was being installed at St John's and All Souls. This can still be seen (although heightened later) at St John's where it was put into the new library, erected in 1597-1601 as a freestanding building on an east/west axis and with a large end window. This was thus the first library specifically designed on the stall system. The bays were however extravagantly wide at ten feet with the result that although the presses were made deeper than required for two folios back to back, the distance between them was still too great for the comfort of readers sitting at fixed benches. The stall system also survives, in a particularly attractive form, at Corpus where the change was probably made in 1604, the college accounts recording the purchase of the necessary locks, bars and chains, together with the dressing and repair of some 640 books. This figure suggests that the library had increased by about a book a month over the past fifteen years. The change to stalls was made in 1602-6 at New College and in 1610-11 at Magdalen and Christ Church.

[14, front cover, 15]

The most striking example of the new stalls is of course Duke Humfrey's Library, the historic centre of what is now the Bodleian. The refurbishing in this manner lay at the heart of Sir Thomas Bodley's restoration of the University or, as it was then termed 'Public', library. The stalls here are eleven and a half feet long, divided into three presses instead of two, and six feet six inches high, divided into three shelves rather than two above the reading desk. Volumes which, when laid on lecterns, occupied seven feet of space, now took up a mere thirty inches of shelving; and where the new stalls had shelves at three levels the capacity of each library bay was increased at least tenfold. Items of particular importance were placed in special cupboards (or 'Grates') with a lattice-work grille in front, while the smaller formats were initially housed in the 'Closets' or librarians' studies at the four corners of the room. The volumes were arranged by subject into Theology, Law, Medicine and Arts, and within each of the further subdivisions into a roughly alphabetical order governed by the initial letter of the surname of the author of the volume, or by the initial letter of the work placed first in it. At the end of each stall a wooden frame contained a 'Table', that is a list of books on the adjacent shelves.

[16-18, frontispiece]

Bodley had first offered to restore the University's library on 23 February 1598 and the library was officially opened on 8 November 1602. Readers of all sorts came in numbers, averaging in the early years as many as seventeen a day, with a fair proportion of foreigners. Bodley himself not only made and encouraged gifts of both books and manuscripts but also, experienced as a former diplomat, arranged for purchases to be made from all over Europe. The rapid flow of books had certain consequences. The rather summary 'Tables', boards with lists of the books in the bay, at the ends of the presses became inadequate as a guide to the contents of the library and the first Librarian, Thomas James (1573-1629), was instructed to make a printed catalogue. Despite the plague of 1603 this was published in 1605, just in time for the visit of King James I, who presented his own works bound, in the fashion of the day, in velvet. The catalogue, the second institutional one to appear in Europe (preceded only by that of Leiden in 1595), contained some ten thousand titles but had to have an appendix to contain the 1,200 items supplied by the London bookseller, John Norton, while it was in the press. By now the space in the studies for books of smaller format, which it was not possible to chain, had already run out and extra shelving had to be provided by the erection of a gallery along the wall at the west end of the library, the first time such a shelving expedient had been used. At this time there were around six thousand volumes in the library, representing however many more individual works since several items were bound together in order to economize on both shelf- and chain-space.

The founder's letters to his librarian show him to be an exact and far-sighted administrator with a firm grip on all aspects of library life. A cleaner was appointed to 'sweep and kepp clean the floor, desks and books', which, as he comments on one occasion was the only way to remedy the 'inconvenience of spitting'. Sweeping and dusting also were to be accompanied by rubbing the floor 'with a little rosemary for a stronger scent I do not like' he wrote, while also stressing the importance of 'tying up', by which he presumably meant dealing with those volumes where the fore-edge silk and string ties had been left undone by readers. In some private libraries of the period dust-repellent pelmets ('valans') were beginning to appear - John Evelyn saw them at Paris in 1644 at the Duke of Orleans' and it should be noted that desks were then covered with a coarse baize (called 'bure' and giving the name 'bureau'). A 'turning desk' is recorded in an Oxford inventory of 1659. On 13 April 1603 Bodley wrote of a more serious problem: 'The breeding of wormes in your deskes, we can not prevent: but for the mouldring of the bookes, it may soone be remedied, if the cleanser of the Librarie doe his duty. For I doe expect at his handes, that for my 4. markes stipend, he should not onely sweepe the Libr[ary] but at the lest twice a quarter, with cleane clothes strike away the dust and mouldring of the bookes: which I am of opinion, will not then continue long, sith nowe it proceedeth chiefly of the newnes of the forrels [= either the covering material generally or, specifically, a covering in a kind of parchment resembling vellum], which in time will be lesse and lesse dankishe.'

In 1610 Bodley made his famous arrangement with the Stationers' Company for the deposit in the library of one perfect copy of every book printed by its members. The Bodleian's lack of space was nevertheless already evident and an extension to the building was under discussion, the first proposal being for an extension of a slightly greater width which would be added on to the east end. A contemporary sketch shows that the stalls were to be continued and to be on the same axis as those in Duke Humfrey, being lit by three more small windows in the new north and south walls. It is likely that Bodley then knew that in the library at the Escorial, built by Philip II of Spain in 1584 (as in the possibly better-known Ambrosian Library at Milan, opened to the public in 1609), free-standing bookcases had been abandoned in favour of wall-shelving and in the final, larger, building (Arts End 1610-13) this new system was adopted for the first time in a new English library building. In Arts End projecting stalls were abandoned for shelving (in fact similar to a half stall) running along the whole of the east and west walls up to the standard stall height. Other plain wall-shelving continued above, on to the (raised) full height of the room, which was lit by both a great east window and two smaller ones at the north and south ends. The books on the three lowest shelves were chained as before and were to be read on the familiar sloping desks; those on the fourth shelf (mainly quartos) were not chained but were protected by locked grilles in front of them (as had been installed at the Ambrosiana in 1603-9).

Those of smaller format on the subsequent higher shelves, reached from galleries supported on timber pillars, were not chained: in other words the press and desk system of the stalls was combined with the former top gallery, giving staff-only access to the smaller formats. The whole of the high wall-space provided there was thus an immediate further gain in shelving. It is possible that the limitations that this put on the fenestration meant that the light therefore available at the desks was insufficient for readers and when a similar extension was added on to the west end in 1634-36 (Selden End) it was given five instead of three large traceried windows (of which two in the west wall were blocked up in 1753). The wall-shelving system thus introduced at the Bodleian in 1610 was however not really taken up by other Oxford libraries until the eighteenth century, virtually all new seventeenth-century libraries continuing the stall system.

[19, 20]

Despite this addition of space in the Bodleian further late seventeenth-century gifts, including in particular that of the library of Thomas Barlow, Bodley's Librarian from 1652 to 1660 and Bishop of Lincoln from 1675 until his death in 1691, necessitated the construction of another gallery, this time over the stalls on the south side of Duke Humfrey. The weight of this soon caused the outer wall to bulge out some seven inches and in 1702 Sir Christopher Wren advised the construction of extended buttresses to withstand the outward thrust.

Sir Thomas Bodley died on 28 January 1613 and the day after his funeral the first stone was laid of the Schools Quadrangle. This provided, on the site of the tumbledown schools to the east of the Divinity School, other university lecturing accommodation and, at Bodley's expense, a third storey right round the three sides of the new quadrangle, which thus afforded the library 'a very large supplement for stowage of Bookes.' Arts End was linked to the new quadrangle by the insertion of two staircases in the corners. Like Arts End itself, these staircases had ribbed outer decoration, the vertical emphasis being taken up by the tracery of the large windows of the new lecture rooms. The crocketted pinnacles of the Gothic Divinity School, taken round the whole quadrangle and springing from the crenellated parapet, helped to unify the mixture of styles. The provision of an imposing tower gateway was achieved by constructing at the centre of the eastern range a tower in the contemporary vogue for the Five Orders of classical architecture and possibly inspired by the similar one at Merton.

[21, 22]

On the inside Bodley's addition, a large open room going round the three sides of the quadrangle and offering enormous potential for book storage, was equally magnificent with a fine painted ceiling (taken down in the 1830s). Below this and above shelf level was a painted frieze where over two hundred heads in medallions alternated with representations of books, manuscripts, scrolls, inkwells, hour-glasses, sundials and globes. The selection of portraits was made by Bodley's first Librarian, Thomas James, and illustrated his personal thesis that from the sub-Apostolic church through the Middle Ages and Reformation up to Jacobean England there had been a continuity of written witness against the pretensions of the Roman Church. They therefore formed a guide to the works to be found on the library's shelves. The sequence is carefully organised, having the Fathers of the Church and theologians on the south side, Medicine and Law around the Tower room, and the Arts, from Homer to Sir Philip Sidney, on the north, the faculty groupings being exactly those into which the library books were classified. The heads were based on contemporary published collections such as Beza's *Icones virorum illustrium*, 1580, and Thevet's *Portraits des hommes illustres*, 1584. Put up between 1616 and 1619, the frieze was covered over in 1830 but rediscovered and restored in 1949. James's other great achievement was to start the series of printed catalogues, the first being published in 1605, and then 1620 (supplement 1635), 1674, 1738, and 1843 (supplement 1851). Many of these became authoritative works and interleaved copies were used in college libraries and elsewhere as a basis for those libraries' own catalogues.

[23, 24]

The mid-sixteenth century was a period in which collections poured in and extra space was soon urgently needed. By 1634 it seems to have been accepted that the old west end entrance should be pulled down, that a grander Convocation House (replacing the room attached to St Mary's) should be built across the east end of the Divinity School (thus creating an H with the Proscholium), and that further library space should be provided above. Thus Arts End, Duke Humfrey's Library, and the 'New End', achieved the shape we know today. The impetus behind all this seems to have been the High Anglicanism generated by William Laud, one of the aims of which was to rid St Mary's of all the secular university functions which it had traditionally housed. The culmination of this was reached after the Civil War by the transfer of the then rather riotous degree ceremonies to the purpose-built Sheldonian Theatre (1669).

The 'New End', as the area was originally known, was of exactly the same length as Arts End but somewhat wider (28 feet), this dimension probably being dictated by the needs of the Convocation House below. The fenestration was the same as that of Arts End, including a central window with cinquefoil lights facing down Duke Humfrey's Library, but with two extra, smaller, windows in the west wall. The wooden furnishings also followed the general pattern of those in Arts End but in a grander, more purposeful and architecturally conscious Jacobean manner. The forty years since Sir Thomas's efforts to lift the 'Public Library' out of its medieval state had seen a notable change in England and the furnishings of the Convocation House, of the intruded disputation furniture in the Divinity School, and of the new library area show the change. The library is still chained, three rows of folios still occupy shelves above a sloping desk, there are still grilled cupboards above, and a gallery for the smaller formats above that. However the seats (even if they lack backs), columns and galleries are all heavier, more ornate, and seem part of the panelled whole. The staircases to the latter are neatly fitted in under the arch from Duke Humfrey's Library and disguised in pedimented cupboards. This lateral access was made possible by bringing the galleries further into the centre of the archway and nearly in line with the ends of the Duke Humfrey stalls. The archway itself is wood encased. Neat framed subject or collection notice boards are part of the panelling. David Loggan's engraving of 1675 shows well both the similarities and the differences. One can sense too the change in atmosphere: Arts End is relatively bare, spartan and even cold, the 1640 development is better lit, more civilized, and even looks warmer. Professor Pevsner sees in all this an early example of the 'Artisan Mannerism' of 1650. This then was the Bodleian that Charles I and his Court would have known when they were in Oxford during the Civil War, just as it was the Bodleian that General Fairfax saved at the conclusion of the siege of Oxford. It was here too that the University entertained Fairfax and Cromwell in 1649 and Charles II in 1663, and where James II breakfasted off a small collation of one hundred and eleven dishes of meat, sweetmeats, and fruit in September 1687.

[25, 26]

A less illustrious scholarly visitor coming to the Bodleian around 1700 would have found that the opening hours were from 8 to 11 a.m. and from 2 to 5 p.m. Readers who were members of the University had to wear their gowns and, at least from 1621 to 1692, foreigners (to the University) had to buy a copy of the printed catalogue. The entrance now was up one of the square staircases projecting into the quadrangle which had been added on as part of the Arts End construction, the west end ones having been demolished in the building of Selden End. The quadrangle entrances to these were only abandoned in the mid-twentieth century and the present central entrance introduced in 1968. Over the head of the stairs was a monitory plaque which, *inter alia*, prohibited the wearing of swords although this may not in fact have been enforced. The six folio volumes of catalogue lay on a table at the east end of Duke Humfrey's Library and were partly in manuscript owing to the great number of recent additions. Reading conditions were uncomfortable, the rooms were not well lit, and at times very cold, the temperature sinking on one occasion when the roof was undergoing repair to eleven degrees below freezing. Nor were the staff notorious for their courtesy. Loggan's 1675 engravings show visitors of either sex looking at the library but tourism on any grand scale only started in the mid-eighteenth century. A 1749 guidebook lists over a dozen 'curiosities' which were usually on display. These included statues, paintings and manuscripts but very few printed books (Cicero, *De Officiis*, Mainz, 1465), attention being centred rather on Chinese pictures, 'a book of Turkish habits' and Archbishop Laud's Mexican hieroglyphs.

Unlike the Bodleian, the colleges were still committed to the stall system and most of those built in the seventeenth century retained this form. The earliest of these is however something of an exception. Erected just before the Civil War, the St John's Laudian library had to fit in with the design of the Canterbury Quadrangle (built 1632-36), being over its arcaded cloister. It was made to abut at a right angle against the Elizabethan library from which access was gained through a fine pedimented doorway. This 'Inner' or 'Mathematical' Library was not so much a reading library as a storage area for both rare or small items and mathematical or scientific instruments and curios. These were housed in cabinets with fine grilled fronts, sadly removed in Victorian times when the present stalls were intruded. College libraries newly built after the Civil War continued to use the stall system. The Brasenose library of 1656, built by the same master mason as the Laudian library at St John's, was also over a cloister, had nine eight-foot bays with stalls, and a general area before the main window where cupboards could house small or rare items. University College (built 1668-72) had both stalls and some galleried higher shelving on the Bodleian (Arts End) model and the same may have been intended at Jesus College (1676-79), as the high fenestration suggests. The small St Edmund Hall Old Library (1675-84) is the only surviving example of a college following closely the new Bodleian example.

[27-30]

Archbishop Laud, as Chancellor of the University, had managed to establish formal University printing at Oxford and the 1636 Royal Charter gave the University the right to appoint three printers. Laud's own gifts of manuscripts, those he encouraged others to give, and the purchase of matrices for Hebrew and Arabic type from Holland, allowed for the appointment of an Architypographus in 1658. In 1668, under the influence of John Fell, Dean of Christ Church and Vice-Chancellor, a proper University Press was set up in the new Theatre that Fell persuaded Archbishop Sheldon to fund. Exotic types were obtained (putting Oxford second only to the Vatican press), a type-foundry and paper-mill were established, and thus the 1670s saw the production in Oxford of the third Bodleian catalogue (1674), Wood's *Historia Universitatis* (1674), Loggan's *Oxonia illustrata* (1675), Prideaux's *Marmora Oxoniensia* (1676), and Plot's *Oxfordshire* (1677). Bernard's union catalogue of manuscripts (1697) attracted attention to local holdings, while the scientific activity here of those associated with the Botanic Garden (1632), with the Wadham group which formed the nucleus of the Royal Society (Wilkins, Boyle, and Hooke in the 1650s), and with the Ashmolean Museum (1683), at last gave Oxford some sort of standing in the scientific world. Small collections of books grew up in some of these departments and around the chairs of geometry and astronomy, but the impact of Oxford science at this period on the Bodleian was probably limited to some remarkable shelves in the Arts End gallery holding a number of presentation copies of works by early members of the Royal Society. There was nonetheless a general rise in communication between scholars, evidenced by the increase in learned periodicals, and, from the time of the Civil War, a shift from Latin to English as the language of print, all of which did much to put the book world into fashion.

The magnificent library at The Queen's College (1692-95) has features in common with these earlier libraries but at the same time it manages to breathe a very different atmosphere and one for which Sir Christopher Wren's great library for Trinity College, Cambridge (1676), must be the inspiration. The library is part of a designed college complex, was originally free-standing, and is over what was, on the east side, an open arcade. This was closed in during the 1840s in order to create a ground floor reading room and to house Robert Mason's notable benefaction. The library has a north/south axis with a grand entrance at the south (now generally disused) and a large window at the north end, but it is still organised on the stall system. The facade is a carefully centralised composition, the floor area is considerable (strictly comparable with Duke Humfrey), and the height is remarkable, allowing for lofty round-headed windows springing from above the stalls. The huge and flat white ceiling is decorated with high quality plasterwork (by James Hands and dated 1695 but with central designs added circa 1756) and reflects the light, showing up the outstanding carved wooden cupboard doors. These were formerly said to be by Grinling Gibbons but more recently have been attributed to Thomas Minn, the joinery contractor for the building. The whole aims clearly at reasonable but not excessive provision on the older basis (the college had inherited those of Bishop Barlow's books which did not go to the Bodleian), but also at architectural effect and, as such, heralds both the style and the ideas of the coming century.

[31]

From Classical to Gothic Inspiration

Classical architecture had been introduced to Oxford with the construction of Wren's Sheldonian Theatre in 1663-69 but when he left the town in the latter year his place as the motivating force in building design passed to two academics, Dean Aldrich (1648-1710) of Christ Church and Dr George Clarke (1661-1736) of All Souls. Aldrich was a polymath who wrote on architecture, designed the University's almanacks and became Vice-Chancellor, while Clarke, after an impressive political career, was for a long time closely associated with much of the building going on in one of Oxford's busiest architectural periods. Notable sums of money were forthcoming to finance new accommodation. Architecture seems, following the reconstruction of London and in line with the development of so many country seats, to have been veritably in fashion. A bilingual (Latin-Italian) edition of Palladio, published by the University Press in 1712 (based on the 1575 and 1596 editions in the Bodleian), attracted a large and impressive list of subscribers. The University erected the Clarendon Building (1711-15) and shortly afterwards Nicholas Hawksmoor, Clarke's architect, could even envisage massive town planning projects balancing a civic forum with an academic forum. Early and mid-eighteenth century High Tory Oxford is often said, following Edward Gibbon's famous strictures, to have been a period of decline, and admissions certainly dropped, but Oxford men largely maintained their place in the governing class of the nation and, in the library world at least, the legacy of earlier Tory favour led to considerable expansion among the colleges.

The library of The Queen's College was the first to be built in the classical style. Its architect is unknown but it is not now thought to have been Dean Aldrich although, among other work, the general plan for the Peckwater Quad at Christ Church was his (the design for the Baroque library there however being Clarke's). The Christ Church development took several decades; the initial designs dating from 1705 but building only beginning in 1717. Largely completed by 1739, it had however to have its ground floor loggia enclosed in 1764, and was thus only finally completed in 1772. The library has a symmetrical plan, turns its back on the south, and faces north on to the quad. The first floor library relies on wall-shelving and galleries for its storage and leaves a positively embarrassing amount of floor space free. The ceiling with its plasterwork by Thomas Roberts is again, as at Queen's, of top quality. The college had received numerous benefactions during the lengthy construction period and eventually the ground floor was enclosed to house another gift of pictures.

[32, 33]

Meanwhile All Souls, where large development plans directed by Clarke and Hawksmoor were also in hand, had in 1710 received news of the bequest to the college not only of the twelve-thousand-volume library of one of its Fellows, Christopher Codrington, one of the richest landowners in the West Indies, but also of £10,000 from his estate to build and endow a new library to house the books. Hawksmoor's passion for symmetry and his respect for substantial Gothic buildings resulted in a plan for a new north quadrangle which placed the library as its northern range, answering to the existing fifteenth-century chapel (plus a new hall to be built on its axis) to the south. The new library, as a result, had a blank ground-floor wall with huge south-facing windows above it and measures just under 200 feet in length (30 in width and 40 in height). Its exterior is faithfully Gothic but its interior is uncompromisingly classical, with Palladian windows at its east and west ends and with two-tier galleried wall-cases (designed by James Gibbs after Hawksmoor's death) on its north side, and with single-tier wall-cases below the windows on the south. The whole library is carried on brick vaults - presumably as a precaution against the damp to which a ground-floor library might be subject. In its vast room the Codrington reader is accommodated at elegant, free-standing, movable, individual sloping desks in the first major English academic library not built on an upper floor.

[34,35]

While Clarke and Hawksmoor were planning the new All Souls, Oxford received yet another bequest, that of the physician to William III, Dr John Radcliffe (1652-1714), who in his lifetime had indicated that he would leave his considerable library and fortune to the University. As early as 1710 therefore plans were being entertained for a notable extension to the Bodleian. At first this took the form of a southern wing to be added to Arts End over part of the Exeter College garden, the college being recompensed with a ground floor college library. It is evident that the architect's brief was for something monumental rather than a building useful as a library and plans soon featured a circular building, the location of which could be either to the west of Selden End, or to the south of Arts End, or even adjacent to the south face of the main block. There were also various proposals for a large rectangular library virtually filling the area between St Mary's and the Schools' quadrangle but these must have been deemed too utilitarian and insufficiently imposing. The project dragged on and it was only after the death of Hawksmoor in 1736 that James Gibbs received the commission, the building being erected between 1737 and 1748. The opening ceremony in 1749 was the occasion for the Vice-Chancellor, Dr William King, to make a highly controversial pro-Jacobite speech. The circular domed structure recalls Italian baroque churches and initially had an open ground floor arcade through which the reader passed to reach the circular cantilevered stairs leading to the first floor library. Here bookcases line the outer walls on both floor and gallery levels while large tables fill the outer ambulatory. It is clear however that book storage capacity was not seen as the prime prerequisite.

The central area of the floor has fine two-colour marble paving and in the late eighteenth century housed numerous classical sculptures.

[36-38]

Clarke equally had a hand in the eighteenth-century developments at Worcester College where the library (1720-33) runs the full length of the central block over the main entrance. It is reached by a spiral stone staircase and has tall wall shelving with a gallery on its west-facing inside wall. The lofty, spacious room with its white bookcases is clearly attractive but Vitruvius's orientational principles have evidently not been followed. As with other eighteenth-century libraries such as All Souls, Oriel and even the Queen's, serious damage has over the years resulted and led to the sunbleached leather bindings. James Wyatt's free-standing Palladian library (1788-94) at Oriel is again on the first floor, over the Common Room. Here too the library faced south but the nature of the fenestration reduces the effects of the sun and light while a fine cupola at the east end focuses the eye which, in other types of room, would be drawn to a fireplace. Wyatt had already remodelled the libraries of New College (1778) and Brasenose (1779-80, blocking up windows) in the classical style and was, at this watershed date, to go on to re-Gothicise several halls as well as to convert one into a library at Balliol.

[39-42]

In putting the emphasis on architecture, and in particular on classical architecture, and in adopting wall cases, the eighteenth century had turned its back on the older chained library. Security was now achieved by ornate grills and it seems likely that colleges changing to new library buildings in the eighteenth century removed the chains from their older books as part of that operation. However in those libraries where the stall system remained, the actual dechaining was a long drawn out matter. Chains were being removed from Cambridge libraries from the 1590s but at Oxford it was only in 1756 that the Bodleian (a public as opposed to a private college library) removed theirs. Purchases of new chains went on well into the second half of the century and deliberate dechaining is only recorded at The Queen's (1780), Balliol (1791), Merton (1792), and, last of all, at Magdalen (1799). George Crabbe, writing his poem *The Library* in 1808, records this shift:

> Ah! needless now this weight of massy chain;
> Safe in themselves, the once-lov'd works remain;
> No readers now invade their still retreat,
> None try to steal them from their parent-seat,
> Like antient beauties they may now discard
> Chains, bolts, and locks, and lie without a guard.

The chain system required that the volume be shelved with its spine innermost on the shelf so that the fore-edge with the staple holding the chain could be on the outer side. Books were therefore often marked with their press number on the fore-edge and, as a consequence, frequently had no lettering on the concealed spine. In the Bodleian at least it seems to have taken some time before the larger and formerly chained volumes were turned round and, perhaps later still and probably just after 1800, lettered. It will be seen that there is a surprising uniformity to most of the spine lettering pieces in, for example, Arts End, where the nature of the leather used and the decorative style show that much of the lettering was done as one general operation.

College libraries had been growing during the eighteenth century partly as a result of college development plans and partly in order to cope with benefactions of books bequeathed by an increasingly book-collecting academic and social world. Few libraries made extensive purchases and for much of the century this was equally true of the Bodleian. The 1710 Copyright Act, which first included the legal concept of copyright in the same act as the need for legal deposit, had little effect although it was probably the existence of the Act which caused John Radcliffe to leave his books and money for the founding of a separate library. From mid-century however major benefactions came thick and fast: the major collections arriving being those of Rawlinson, St Amand, Clarendon, Carte, and Godwyn. Both the size and the condition of some of these gifts could cause problems - as benefactions do occasionally to this day. Some of Tanner's books fell into the Thames from the barge in which they were being transported and Roger Dodsworth's manuscripts were so wet on arrival that they had to be aired for the whole of the sunny month of July 1675 on the leads of the library roof. Space became once again a problem, especially since the Library still contained many items today viewed more as museum pieces and which included the numerous paintings in the Picture Gallery (today the Upper Reading Room) and the Arundel marbles. In 1749 the marbles were moved to the ground floor and the Picture Gallery was wainscotted. Shortly afterwards two of the three west windows in Selden End were blocked up and in 1766 the benches between the Duke Humfrey stalls were removed and Windsor chairs substituted. In 1780 a remedy was found for the Library's lack of purchasing income by charging readers for the use of the Library and by allocating to it a part of the University's matriculation fees. This allowed the Bodleian to make important purchases at some of the major sales of the 1790s, such as Crevenna and Pinelli. In 1787 the former Anatomy School in the south west corner of the first floor was handed over to the Library and marked the first stage in its progressive taking over of the whole complex. This room, termed the Auctarium (today housing the catalogue), was refurbished by Wyatt with elegant wire-fronted bookcases.

The Age of Reform
The substitution of chairs for benches was a gesture towards readers but in general terms working conditions in the libraries in 1800 remained roughly what they had been for virtually three hundred years; that is, there was no heating and no artificial light - in some ways ideal storage conditions for books and manuscripts. In the Bodleian opening hours were from 10 a.m. to 3 p.m. in winter and from 9 a.m. to 4 p.m. in summer although one reader summed the conditions up by saying that he would work there all day 'or for as long as I can stand it'. In 1831 Bodley was recorded as having a daily average of three or four readers and in July of that year there were none at all for the whole month. As far as the books and manuscripts were concerned

therefore a lack of wear and tear was to be added to the excellence of the storage. In all these respects however things were to change considerably in the coming decades. Already in 1821 the Curators of the Bodleian had introduced the new hot air heating in Selden End, fed by a boiler housed in an extra buttress on the north side of the Convocation House. The Bodleian orator of the day commended the innovation but hoped, in a far-sighted anticipation of the effects of central heating, that it would not send readers to sleep. It is not known whether he foresaw the effects on the books. Further modernisation came with the introduction of steam heating pipes in the Bodleian in 1845 (altered to hot water in 1857), the timber beams under Duke Humfrey's having to be cut into in order for the pipes to pass along.

The first three decades of the nineteenth century saw the arrival in Bodley of three major bequests: those of Gough (1809), Malone (1821), and Douce (1834). The first floor 'schools' or lecture rooms were progressively allocated to the Library and, with the construction of the University and Randolph Galleries in 1845 (today the Ashmolean Museum), the top floor Picture Gallery could be cleared of some pictures and made available at least in part. Space remained a problem and on both sides of the quad the northern windows were blocked by shelves. Moreover if the spate of bequests which had characterized the great bibliophile era of the late eighteenth and early nineteenth centuries was still continuing, the progressive tightening of the mechanism of legal deposit was increasing the annual intake of the Library in a notable manner. The 1836 Copyright Act had reduced the number of deposit libraries from the nine (later eleven) created in 1710 to five but the Act of 1842 made deposit in the British Museum obligatory, doubling the intake there, and accessions also grew elsewhere. The Bodleian and the other major legal deposit libraries set up their own mechanism for claiming and the former's intake rose from 2,400 volumes a year in 1842 to 30,000 by the year 1882. As a result the total printed book stock rose from a quarter of a million in 1850 to half a million in the mid-eighteen eighties and to one million by the outbreak of the First World War.

[43]

From the start Bodleian books had been classified into four major groups according to the traditional faculties (Theology, Law, Medicine, Arts) and subdivided within each group by format, although large private benefactions were usually kept together. Spatial pressures progressively made the clear separation and location of these subject collections very difficult and by the early nineteenth century the system had largely broken down. In 1824 a new classification was introduced for the legal deposit intake, these 'yearbooks' being based on the alphabetical ordering and numeration of such intake every six months. In the light of general developments in the library world this was eventually abandoned and in 1862 an in-house numerical subject classification introduced. However subject classification is of less use when there is no access to the shelves and it requires more shelf space if there are to be enough growing points at which new books can be inserted. Now that the computer-based catalogue can provide subject access the Bodleian has reverted to a tight-packed shelving system reminiscent of the yearbook one.

The long and complex struggle to find more space turned in part on the building of the new University Press premises in Walton Street (1831, thus freeing the Clarendon Building), on the creation of the University Museum in 1860, on the University's progressive transfer of many museum-type collections to the University Galleries in Beaumont Street (which adopted the Ashmolean name only in 1899), and by the decision to transfer University teaching to a High Street site by the building of the Examination Schools (1882). The latter incidentally had only just won the day over the suggestion of retaining the Schools quadrangle for the traditional purpose of lecturing and of moving the Bodleian to the High Street site. Other plans discussed in the 1870s included filling in the main quadrangle with a steel structure containing book storage below and a reading room above, stripping Duke Humfrey's Library for use as a reading room, and taking over both the Divinity School and the Convocation House for the library. Other permanent worries were the risk of fire (for which walls across the longer rooms and iron doors were seen as the solution) and the structural weakness of the Old Library building. Plans were considered (1858) for filling the main body of the building with an iron structure capable of taking the weight of the books and the bookshelves, but in the end the wooden floors and bookcases were retained.

Late eighteenth-century criticisms of Oxford's academic contribution grew considerably in the early nineteenth century. Despite the introduction of Honour Schools in 1801 and the attempts of some colleges to improve their tutorial record, these were strengthened rather than dispelled by the backward looking nature of some members of the Tractarian or 'Oxford' Movement in the 1830s and 1840s although Newman himself was a leading proponent of the tutorial system and of educational reform. Public opinion, having instituted change in the parliamentary system, was thus about to demand change in the University too: the 1854 University Reform Act, following on after the Royal Commission of 1850, remodelled the University constitution, opened more Fellowships to laymen, encouraged new Honours Schools, and paved the way for the advent of more liberal-minded men. As a result the Bodleian statute was altered in 1856 to allow the limited admission of undergraduates, a move which soon led to the transfer of the Radcliffe Library to the Bodleian and the establishment in 1861 of the Radcliffe Camera (still only on the first floor) as a reading room for students. Within two years the open colonnaded ground floor was enclosed by windows, furnished, and the present staircase and entrance added on the north side. Central provision for the student body thus took shape and by 1878 daily maximum attendance at the Camera was 130, rising by 1880 to 275 on a winter's day. By 1920 this figure was well over 500. In 1941 the ground floor was opened up as a reading room. Gas lighting had been installed in the Camera in 1835, being provided by bronze pillar lamps on the gallery balcony and by a nine-branched standard in the centre of the room. The fine marble floor was covered with coconut matting to deaden the sound of readers' boots. These concessions to modernity were justified by the thought that, should fire break out, the Camera, being a free-standing building, would not seriously endanger the Old Bodleian, threatened as the latter had been by the burning down of the nearby Exeter College library in 1709, one of perhaps only two cases of a serious Oxford library fire. Security against fire was indeed a constant curatorial worry from the late 1840s on and various solutions were discussed. These included the use of the Proscholium and even Galton's proposal of 1874 to build a three storey fire-proof block right across the Schools Quadrangle, dividing it into two small wells. In the end the Curators went no further than to insulate the heating pipes and to install an iron door to Duke Humfrey's Library.

[46]

The number of purpose-built new libraries put up in the nineteenth century was rather limited. The first, and almost the only University library, to be erected was that of the Taylor Institution, a centre for the teaching of the modern European languages but where, since the University did not examine these formally, the library provided the principal function. The bequest of Sir Robert Taylor (1714-88) had only reached the University in 1835, at the same time as funds for the creation of a sculpture gallery. Further moneys being added from the profits of the University Press, a joint building was constructed by C.R. Cockerell after an architectural competition. It has been described as Oxford's last classical building and one of the cleverest, for it houses two completely separate institutions and yet appears externally as an harmonious unit. The Taylorian (entitled 'Institutio Tayloriana' on the front) stands on the east. The St Giles' facade, recalling something of a triumphal arch, houses, in the centre of the first floor, the magnificent main reading room. This is still a first floor library but it is the earliest in Oxford to have had fireplaces installed from the start in every room. The classical interior, the originally grilled main-floor wall-bays, and the octagonal gallery with semi-dome give a remarkable sense of space and ease. The east/west window orientation allows for fine views but causes excessive light exposure to some shelves for which blinds were the only answer – a viable system so long as, throughout the nineteenth century, this remained little more than a clubbable research library. Today these problems have to be resolved by the use of ultra-violet filters on the window panes. The environmental problems here were exacerbated, beyond the open fires and later additional central heating, by gas lighting, the dire effects of which on leather bindings were only generally realized at the beginning of the twentieth century.

[44, 45]

The University had however gradually been forced to open itself to change, to modernise its courses, to abandon its traditional restrictions in matters of religion and, in some degree, to make itself more accountable. The number of serious students increased and some attempt to make library provision for them was made: the pace of change may have seemed remarkable at the time but, retrospectively, looks to the modern eye to have been incredibly slow. Despite the Bodleian's provision in the Camera the Union Society library was in fact to be the major resource for many undergraduates for the rest of the century since the colleges were slow to meet undergraduates' needs. College libraries long remained as the Fellows' preserve although some allowed borrowing for loan to pupils. University College, exceptionally, had an undergraduate library in the late eighteenth century but Merton admitted its own undergraduates to its library for but one hour a week in 1827, extending this to three hours daily only in 1899, while in 1902 Oriel still provided no more than a cupboard full of books for students. Separate undergraduate library rooms existed however in Jesus in 1865, in Balliol in 1871, in Trinity in 1877 and in Pembroke and Christ Church in the 1880s.

[48, 49]

Equally no new college libraries were built in the first half of the nineteenth century although the situation changed notably thereafter. The first to be put up was that at Exeter which was built as a separate structure in the garden in 1856. Designed by George Gilbert Scott, it kept up the medieval tradition of closely spaced library windows and had a polygonal stone stair-turret and timber vaulting on the upper floor. Scott's library for University College five years later has tall windows and Italianate elements but has had to be divided horizontally to make more space. The original library of the Oxford Union Society was designed in 1863 by William Wilkinson, the architect of the Randolph Hotel and of many of the Gothic houses on the Norham Manor estate. Here the windows had dogtooth surrounds, the decoration was in vitrified dark blue brick and the main window was decorated with foliage and the head of Shakespeare. The library was subsequently moved into the old debating hall with its famous Pre-Raphaelite decoration. William Butterfield's lofty library at Keble College (1878) is part of his very particular Gothic Revival design for the college, red brick with polychrome patterns in buff stone and coloured brick. The library walls have exposed brickwork, the ceiling is panelled and there are wooden screens to the stacks, all by the architect. Twenty years later two more new foundations – or religiously inspired institutions newly transferred to Oxford – continued the Gothic theme. At Mansfield College Basil Champneys' Perpendicular buildings include a spacious and attractive library whose roof, with its painted panels, is supported by a whole range of posts and beams, all of which gives it considerable character – even if we may now be tempted to consider this style as rather affected. Manchester College, built four years later in 1893, is Thomas Worthington's more conventional contribution, being lofty and well lit; it is better known perhaps for its remarkable contents.

[47, 50-51]

The general pressures built up by changing reading habits, by increasing publication, and by the presence of a more active University were evidently at work in the city too. Following the availability of certain materials earlier in coffee houses, circulating libraries and reading rooms made a regular appearence in Oxford from the mid-1780s when James Fletcher's was established. This was followed by the Oxford Subscription Library in 1809 and that of the University, City and County Reading Rooms in 1823, of which, despite the title, four fifths of the membership were members of the University. Significantly perhaps the Oxford Union Society was founded in the same year and established its library in 1830. The Public Libraries Act was passed in 1850 and Oxford promptly took advantage of it. A general public library was opened in Oxford in 1854 and its popularity with the local population was such that over 100,000 people visited it in its first year so that it had to be kept open for ten hours a day. At this stage the library, of which the first Librarian was B.H. Blackwell (whose son founded the bookshop of the same name), consisted only of reference and reading rooms but a lending section was opened in 1857 and issued over 13,000 books in its first year.

[52, 53, 67]

With the turn of the century however a new period of great activity in library building in Oxford was ushered in, reflecting the improved teaching and the new emphasis on research fostered both by the 1877 University Reform Act and by growing competition from other universities. Science departments, museums and arts faculties alike started small subject-centered libraries, mainly for their own students and based on the influential German seminar library pattern. These occupied rooms in the relevant departments and have been much moved around and extended in different ways, many originally consisting of tall wall cases with open but grilled and lockable fronts. The decade leading up to the First World War was particularly active, seeing such collections starting in geography, classics, philosophy, forestry, agriculture, modern history, agricultural economics, and English language and literature.

The nineteenth century had seen the rise of librarianship as a professional career with the publication, in France and Germany, of manuals of library economy. In Oxford it was suggested in 1868 that *Bibliothekswissenschaft*, the science of libraries, should be taught as part of the University syllabus and that All Souls should become a college of which Bodley's Librarian should be Warden and the Bodleian staff should be Fellows. Despite the failure of this plan the Library Association held its first meeting in Oxford in 1878 (presided over by its first President, H.O. Coxe, Bodley's Librarian) and in its early days was closely linked with the University's librarians before becoming more connected with the public library movement. Since then the University's libraries have, for many years, seen a number of Oxford librarians move on to hold distinguished posts elsewhere. In 1902 E.W.B. Nicholson, Bodley's Librarian, an exceptional manager and trainer, started a Staff Kalendar, a series of instructional handbooks which continued for some sixty years and gave not only the routines and duties for each day of the year but also the regulations concerning junior staff, the chief duties of seniors, 'regulations for the good order of rooms', rules for 'counting', rules for the catalogues, for labelling and lettering, and an index of library forms, to name only some. The daily duties identified those responsible for such tasks as the winding of clocks, the cleaning of specified areas, the provision of administrative reports and statistics, the clearing of gutters, the paying of bills, the filling of fire buckets, the locking up of dead cheques, the drawing of blinds, the repairing of mats and even the oiling of the hinges of the great gate. By 1913 the Bodleian staff numbered 68 persons and its organisation, that of the largest department in the University, was evidently both of considerable complexity and vastly different from what it had been a hundred years before.

The Twentieth Century

By the turn of the century the need for space was urgent as shelving and books were spread all over the Old Bodleian, in the Old Ashmolean building, in the basements of the Sheldonian and the Examination Schools and in the Radcliffe Camera. After some discussion a special underground basement was constructed in 1912 between the Old Library and the Camera. Here two floors, supported on an open iron structure, were equipped with compact rolling shelving, heavy metal cases of a type first used in the British Museum Library in 1887 but radically improved, following new suggestions by W.E. Gladstone, and a type of storage which had been foreseen as providing sufficient space for the legal deposit holdings for many years to come.

By the late nineteen-twenties however there was disenchantment with this system and the need for radical action was accepted. Thanks to the generosity of the Rockerfeller Foundation, development plans could be discussed. Many suggestions, old and new, were brought forward: more underground storage, both north of the Old Library and south of the Camera, the displacement of the University Registry to the north of Broad Street and the taking over of the Clarendon Building, the creation of an out-of-town repository at Wolvercote and even the transplanting of the whole university library to the University Parks. Besides the spatial needs for both storage and administration, there was strong pressure for easier access to material in the 'modern humanities' (the social sciences in particular) and for research and graduate teaching rooms in proximity to the relevant stacks. Here it must be remembered that until 1926 there was no electricity in the Old Bodleian, a fact which radically curtailed both its hours and services. The environmental needs of Bodley's historic collections were also well understood, perhaps a direct result both of the chaotic existing storage conditions and of the almost military methods of internal economy. As a result a compromise solution was reached. The New Bodleian was built, being completed in 1939 just as World War II was breaking out. It provided generous modern storage, administrative space, carrels and study rooms in proximity to the stacks for senior readers. A book service brought materials by means of an underground conveyor belt system to the Old Library reading rooms. These, in their turn, were to be restored, thus satisfying the demands of those unwilling to abandon (as at Cambridge) the traditional site. The transportation by mechanical means (in practice in wooden boxes on a conveyor) of not only modern books but also many valuable, older and fragile manuscripts and books necessarily treats them as mere production items. This, allied to the scale of readers' requests, has therefore given rise to some of the new conservation problems of large libraries such as the wear arising from complex handling and frequent consultation. Reserve storage out of town was also to be built and a revised catalogue was to make the whole stock accessible. On the environmental side it was aimed to provide the New Library stacks with constant temperatures of 55-62 degrees and a humidity of 50-60%, a far-sighted understanding of library needs in this respect at least. An increase in the format breakdown of each classification number to seven different height sizes was calculated to bring a great saving in space. The adjustable metal shelving provided to hold, it was said, five million volumes was however not on the compact (mobile shelving) basis but - ever optimistically - of the open-corridor type, perhaps because of the scale and weight of the structure involved, perhaps also because of the idea of open access which was being discussed as a possibility for senior readers. In the end the library turned its back on such access in the 1950s and by the seventies the spatial problems had again become so severe that compact shelving had to be installed on the then still unshelved bottom floor.

The New Bodleian, designed by Sir Giles Gilbert Scott, has received little praise as architecture, being described as 'neither one thing nor the other, neither in an Oxford tradition nor modern for its date'. Neither neo-Georgian nor Cotswold, it has Dutch Modernist window proportions, neo-baroque portals of the late seventeenth century, and discrete decorations of a municipal style. It can nevertheless be said to place its central core of a pyramid of eleven storage floors unobtrusively into an architecturally very important area and yet to achieve a certain monumentality with its bold horizontal lines. A large steel structure, one of the first of its kind in Oxford and copied from American examples, it stands back somewhat from the street and concedes an important curved corner. The Bladon stone gives both a certain standing and a mellowness which tones in with the surroundings. The interior is perhaps less successful. The Library's collections were transferred to the building during the war period and the New Library was officially opened in 1946, thus allowing the Old Library complex to be restored and reorganised during the next fifteen or so years. Numerous antiquarian discoveries were made in the process of these important works (directed by J.N.L. Myres, an eminent archeologist and then Bodley's Librarian), the most notable being the discovery of the shadows of the fifteenth-century cases in Duke Humfrey's Library, the re-appearance of the portrait frieze in the Upper Reading Room, and the careful restoration of the Duke Humfrey stall cases.

[60, 61]

Unfortunately post-war pressures delayed the out-of-town further storage and completely negated the principle of access for graduate readers, thereby both throwing an excessive strain on the conveyor-belt system (and therefore on the books carried by it) and, because of the delays thus engendered, leading to the rapid development of duplication in other Oxford libraries where the stock was kept on open access. The opening hours of the old Bodleian were extended in 1958 from 7 to 10 p.m. (particularly to help lawyers for whom, with long runs of cases needed for reference, borrowing is less useful), but even this was insufficient. The dramatic escalation of research in the humanities, both in the University and elsewhere (resulting not only in a notable rise in the number of Oxford graduate students but also in extraordinary numbers of academic visitors wishing to use the Bodleian's materials), has thrown a considerable strain on a system designed for far less heavy use. Excessive service demands have thus undermined the advantages of good and potentially open-access storage, the nature of which has also been recently complicated by the fire-prevention restrictions imposed by law to protect staff.

The colleges had also recognized the need to provide for their students and back in the eighteen-nineties Professor Henry Nettleship had encouraged the Society of Oxford Home Students (later St Anne's College) to provide library facilities for all women students in the University. As they established themselves the ladies' colleges regularly included libraries in their building plans, Somerville in 1902 (Champneys),

26

Lady Margaret Hall in 1910 (Blomfield) and again in 1961 (Erith) and St Hugh's in 1936, all providing the standard combination of cosy book bays with work tables between. Lincoln, Trinity and New College all built new libraries, in 1906, 1925 and 1939 respectively, but the most unusual departure was the book tower provided for Nuffield College, a graduate research college, which though designed in 1939 was only completed in 1960. The conversion of redundant chapels and other buildings into college libraries goes back a long way since Exeter College had done this in the seventeenth century but, significantly perhaps, it became more common in the twentieth. Hertford converted its former chapel into a library in 1909, Magdalen College converted Buckler's Boys School in 1932, St Edmund Hall economically took over St Peter-in-the-East, a Romanesque and Gothic structure which is perhaps the most interesting church in Oxford, in 1970, and Lincoln converted All Saints in rather grand style in 1974. These exercises were ingenious but necessarily tell one more about religious history and college expansionism than about library design. Similarly the University rehoused the Social Studies Faculty Library in the old Oxford City Boys High School in 1978.

[55, 57–59, 63, 68]

The redevelopment of the Old Bodleian and the construction of the New were essentially concerned with provision for the humanities. Officially modern science in Oxford dates back to 1850 when the Honour School of Natural Science was inaugurated, but college laboratories dominated the scene until the turn of the century. The Radcliffe Science Library, opened in 1903 and, taking its inspiration from John Radcliffe's scientific books now incorporated in the Bodleian, became, in succession to the University Museum with its rather Gothic setting for science, the focus for what was to emerge as the Science area. From the middle twenties in particular laboratory after laboratory went up, distinguished work was done and Nobel Prizes and other distinctions gained. The cost of science, a University responsibility with regard to buildings and equipment, also had the result of causing the University to become dependent on government funding. The 'RSL' extension, by Sir Hubert Worthington, dates from 1934 but further demands in this field led to a large reading and storage complex, placed under part of the University Museum lawn, and constructed in 1975.

[54, 69]

Radcliffe's books and those scientific publications collected up to the First World War were essentially monographs but as twentieth-century science expanded rapidly it was periodicals, used more briefly for the articles they contained, which became the basic information source. Rapid consultation, borrowing, and later photocopying, replaced the arts reader's long sessions at the desk. The presence of Radcliffe's scientific books in the University Museum in the second half of the nineteenth century had established the right of 'scientists' (that is the museum staff) to have such books in their offices and this form of borrowing for bench-work purposes has remained, being the oldest borrowing privilege in any part of the Bodleian. Nevertheless most laboratories and scientific departments have established their own, sometimes very specialist, libraries, a provision which has, to some extent, been co-ordinated with that of the

Radcliffe Science Library by a general advisory committee in recent years. More recently plans have been made for the Bodleian to deposit (or 'outhouse') some of its relevant legal deposit books in science with certain departmental libraries for a period of time, such works having a limited immediate shelflife. Many departments being essentially research based and undergraduate provision in the colleges being irregular in this expensive field, the Hooke Lending Library was established in a wing of the Radcliffe Science Library in 1972 to meet undergraduate borrowing needs.

[62]

The hiving off of science was accompanied in 1929 by the establishment, across South Parks Road, of Rhodes House as a centre for American and Commonwealth affairs, built complete with its library which, coming at a period when Oxford's library provision was briefly being seen as a whole, was from the start to be a formal part of the Bodleian. Here in an eclectic amalgam, marble, classical rotunda (a memorial to Lord Milner), medieval hall, Arts and Crafts and Cotswold stone styles are joined to a colonial sense of space and to a liberal use of unadorned wood, designed to recall an Imperial form of the gentleman's library. The slightly earlier Indian Institute building (Champneys 1884-96, now housing the History Faculty Library) was in the Jacobean style with a few symbolic references to the India of the Raj. The reorganisation of the Bodleian after World War II included the extrusion of its law section which was housed, together with other libraries, in Sir Leslie Martin's and Colin St John Wilson's St Cross Building (1964). A low, spreading cubic building of sand-coloured brick, it is disposed around a wide, central staircase, rising like an Inca temple. Despite its three-part nature it is an impressive and compact building which fits well into its site, all simply detailed with buff bricks and pale woodwork which, as Diane Kay points out, give a blond Scandinavian feel to the building. Internally the reading areas are light, there are numerous carrels and separate stack areas. It has been described as being the only recent University building of international calibre and as having 'the splendour of Persepolis'. Its strangeness comes from the lack of logic in the brief given to the architects as the building contains three bodies brought together more by their contemporaneous need for accommodation than by congruity of subject; it houses the Bodleian's Law Library, the Institute of Economics and Statistics and the English Faculty with its library.

[56, 64-66]

The building of large new libraries in central Oxford was still being contemplated in the late 1960s but the major world oil crises of the next few years have so far precluded further action. More recently attention has been paid to the creation of small specialist centres such as those for Japanese, Chinese, and, now being planned, for American studies. With legal deposit and constant foreign purchases there is nevertheless a regular demand for storage space and of recent years this has been obtained by the creation of a book repository. This is for the use of the central 'retention' libraries only and is housed eight miles out of Oxford in University-owned parkland at Nuneham Courtenay. Here low areas of air-conditioned compact shelving with minimal lighting provide excellent, if distant, storage from which a daily van service brings items in to Oxford.

Planning permission and finance allowing, further 'modules' can be constructed, one being needed every three or so years if the present permanent retention policies of the central University libraries are to be met. The new media of the late twentieth century, microfilm, tape and computer-based facilities, are also in widespread use throughout the University but, as yet, there is no real sign that the flow of books, or the demand for them, is diminishing.

[70, 71]

The Oxford Library Information Service (OLIS) database, inaugurated (somewhat later than equivalent schemes) in 1988, is in the process of providing the numerous libraries in the University with a single union catalogue, accessible in many ways, such as has been sought since the seventeenth century at least. There is every sign that, as this reveals further the riches of Oxford's stock by making them apparent to subject-based searches, demand, from both local readers and from others elsewhere, both nationally and world-wide, will grow exponentially. This is already putting remarkable strain on a library system evolved over the centuries and most recently planned and built for in the late nineteen-twenties, but now in a very different world, at least as regards access, service and conservation.

Nor are printed books (and for this term read also maps, pamphlets, newspapers etc) the only information items stored in Oxford. Associated with these materials are also the numerous archives or working papers both of the University, and of the colleges and many other bodies. Among these papers there is much important historical material, some dealing with property, some (such as the Conservative Party archive and Sir Harold Wilson's papers) with politics, others, such as the Modern Scientific Archives project (dealing with the papers of great scientists), with the very bases of modern life, be they the evolution of nuclear power, the discovery of penicillin or the advances of molecular biophysics. Some of these papers are housed in colleges, and are still thought of as the older records of the bursar's office or else the personal papers of former members. Such documents, like the manuscripts and printed books which form the core of the great libraries, have been stored, some for centuries, in Oxford buildings.

The city and the University, both built from the start on a raised spit of higher land, have been spared floods and serious fires. The hazards of history have dealt kindly with Oxford: both Royalists and Parliamentarians spared Oxford's libraries the worst of fates as did the bombing raids of the Second World War, to name but some dangers. Minor local problems have of course arisen in all libraries and colleges: as we have seen, books have arrived wet (or, from abroad, contaminated by moulds) and almost every winter some library suffers from the entry of water into an ancient building. Coping with such problems - it is difficult to class any of them as 'disasters' in any way approaching the 1966 Florence flood, the 1988 St Petersburg fire or the 1994 Norwich one - has nevertheless to be envisaged and mutual help in emergency now turns upon the expertise of the Bodleian's Conservation section, created in 1978. Traditionally Oxford libraries had their books bound by local binders who, from the thirteenth century on, were located in Catte Street where the Radcliffe Camera now stands. The trade flourished and, at least in the late seventeenth and early eighteenth centuries, Oxford binders were among the finest in the country. Since at least 1864 the Bodleian has employed its own binders although some of its books and many from other Oxford libraries now go to binders both in Oxford and elsewhere in the United Kingdom.

In general however the quality of both book production and commercial binding has declined, under economic pressures, in recent years, neither the methods of work nor the standards of the materials employed guaranteeing protection to the book for any substantial length of time. Storage in bookstacks heated (in part under the Offices, Shops and Railway Premises Act of 1963) to a level suitable for people (16° centigrade) does not help preserve medieval manuscripts or older books whose parchment and leather become brittle or stiff although recent research has shown that this problem has probably been less serious in Oxford than in, for example, highly heated American libraries. Nevertheless the greatest peril these items face is that of a use which has increased out of recognition in the last century. In the Bodleian where in the early nineteenth century virtually no books were consulted in a month, today thousands are ordered up, handled and read every day. In 1605 the Bodleian was one of the first university libraries to publish a general catalogue of its holdings. All Oxford's riches will soon be available on OLIS and thus eventually traceable nationally, and even internationally, through the automated Joint Academic Network (JANET). Even more scholars will then wish to come to Oxford and to see, consult and read them, thus increasing the physical demands on what are often old and weak structures. Photocopying adds to these strains. Handling, reading, studying and copying procedures have yet to be evolved to cope with these demands – one of Oxford's most urgent problems.

This survey of the history of Oxford's many libraries has dealt with them as places for the storage and the study of books. These functions are both complementary and, at least at times and in certain ways, inimical to each other, representing at their extremes, the 'museum' on one side and the immediate reading needs of the, admittedly academic, public on the other. Besides these storage and study functions there is however a third, and often limiting, element in that the library setting is itself often both a part of the architectural heritage and, as such, an important material witness to the history of the general heritage. This makes these libraries an essential force in the very understanding of many of the volumes forming part of them. The problems arising from the necessary attempt to reconcile these functions have always been considerable: the shift from lectern to stall was doubtless keenly debated and had to be funded, the changes of the seventeenth, nineteenth and earlier twentieth centuries have similarly engendered discussion – nor, in some ways, are these purely Oxford problems, being indeed both national, and even general, cultural ones pertaining to Western philosophy, technological invention and social evolution. In Oxford, then, a rare combination of circumstances allows the Middle Ages, the Renaissance, the Civil War, the Enlightenment, the Romantic Age and that of Reform, as well as the later industrial and technological ones, all to be seen as part of the slow elaboration of

Western culture. It is therefore both Oxford's (and perhaps the nation's) privilege, and its duty, to maintain and to continue these important 'arks for learning', to adapt Francis Bacon's description of the Bodleian, with their delicate balance between their books, their buildings and their constantly evolving functions, all of them vital to the spiritual and intellectual life of each age, past, present – and future.

BIBLIOGRAPHY

The foregoing text has relied more particularly on the following books, at times quoting brief passages verbatim. In order to produce a compact survey full references have been omitted but this in no way diminishes the author's recognition either of his debt to these previous writers or his appreciation of their work.

Bodley, Sir Thomas *The Letters of Sir Thomas Bodley to Thomas James*, ed. G.W. Wheeler. 1926

Clark, J.W. *The care of books.* 1901

Colvin, H.M. *Unbuilt Oxford.* 1983

Cordeaux, E.H. & Merry, D.H. *A bibliography of printed works relating to University of Oxford.* 1968

Craster, Sir Edmund *A History of the Bodleian Library, 1845-1945.* 1952

Craster, Sir Edmund *The History of All Souls College library.* 1971

Gibbs, J. *Bibliotheca Radcliviana.* 1747

Gillam, S.G. *The Divinity School and Duke Humfrey's Library at Oxford.* 1988

Gillam, S.G. *The Radcliffe Camera* (Bodleian picture books, new series 1). 1992

Hibbert, C. ed. *The Encyclopaedia of Oxford.* 1988

Hiscock, W.G. *A Christ Church miscellany.* 1946

Kay, D. "Architecture", *The History of the University of Oxford*, vol. VIII (The twentieth century), ed. B. Harrison, 1994, pp.499–518.

Ker, N.R. *Oxford college libraries in 1556.* 1956

Ker, N.R. *Books, collectors and libraries.* 1985

Ker, N.R. "The Provision of Books", *The History of the University of Oxford*, vol. III (The Collegiate University), ed. J.K. McConica, 1986, pp.441–520.

Macray, W.D. *Annals of the Bodleian Library.* 2nd ed. 1890

Milne, J.G. *The early history of Corpus Christi College.* 1946

Morgan, P. *Oxford libraries outside the Bodleian.* 2nd ed. 1980

Morgan, P. "Oxford college libraries in the eighteenth century", *The Bodleian library record*, XIV, 1992, pp.228–236.

Myres, J.N.L. "Oxford libraries in the seventeenth and eighteenth centuries", *The English library before 1700*, ed. F. Wormald & C.E. Wright, 1958, pp.236–55.

Newman, J. "Oxford libraries before 1800", Royal archaeological Institute, Summer meeting programme, 1978, pp.17–24.

Parkes, M.B. "The Provision of Books", *The History of the University of Oxford*, vol. II (Late medieval Oxford), ed. J.I. Catto and T.A.R. Evans, 1992, pp.407–484.

Philip, I.G. *The Bodleian Library in the seventeenth and eighteenth centuries.* 1983

Powicke, Sir F.M. *The medieval books of Merton College.* 1931

Rogers, D.M. *The Bodleian Library and its treasures 1320-1700.* 1991

Sherwood, J. & Pevsner, N. *Oxfordshire* (The Buildings of England) 1974

Streeter, B.H. *The Chained library.* 1931

See also the appropriate sections of the relevant volumes of the Royal Commission on Historic Monuments and the Victoria County History.

Oxford University Library Statistics 1992–93

Libraries	Books p.a.	Current periodicals.	Total books	Shelfspace l.m.	Seats	Staff
A. *Major libraries*						
Bodleian	74,262	53,750	5,768,175	172,380	2,188	401
Taylorian	7,018	1,147	438,014	13,165	164	20
Ashmolean	2,538	1,270	203,050	5,774	135	12
Economics & Statistics	461	1,955	119,900	2,439	100	5
B. *Humanities Faculty libraries*						
23 libraries	16,627	2,771	663,151	17,401	977	56
C. *Science Department libraries*						
29 libraries	7,513	5,508	440,608	14,916	973	47
D. *College libraries*	36,207	4,868	[?2,000,000]	[?60,000]	2,311	[N/A]
Total	144,626	71,269	?9,632,898	?286,075	6,848	541

Notes: The books figure is for printed monographs only; books p.a. is for books (monographs) acquired in year; current periodicals is number subscribed in year; shelfspace occupied in linear metres is for all materials (i.e. it will include printed books, periodicals, manuscripts, maps etc.). The figures in columns 4 and 5 are estimates and not exact figures. On account of the different classes of material included in column 5, no conclusions as to density should be made by relating columns 4 and 5. All figures are therefore given only as a general indication of the amounts involved in the various fields.

Plates

1   Library chest, Merton College. Late 13th- or 14th-century hutch type in oak, with scrolled ends to the iron straps and three locks. The chest measures two feet by two feet and is five feet long. It stands ten inches off the ground. The triple locks were not only to make it more difficult to force but also to require three authorized keyholders to be present. It is not known how books, kept in the chest either for safety or while on deposit against a cash loan, were stored, although the presence of ears (or lugs) on certain early bindings may suggest that they were placed fore-edge down. The college records refer in 1327 to a 'cista pro libris dialecticis'.

2   Old Library, St Mary the Virgin, 1320s. Sketch by T.G. Jackson in his *The Church of St Mary the Virgin, Oxford* (Oxford, 1897, p.101) showing traces of original narrow windows on the south wall between which the lecterns would have stood. Window interval (and thus double-sided lectern and reader space) about eight feet. The University's original meeting house for its Convocation, or parliament, lies below.

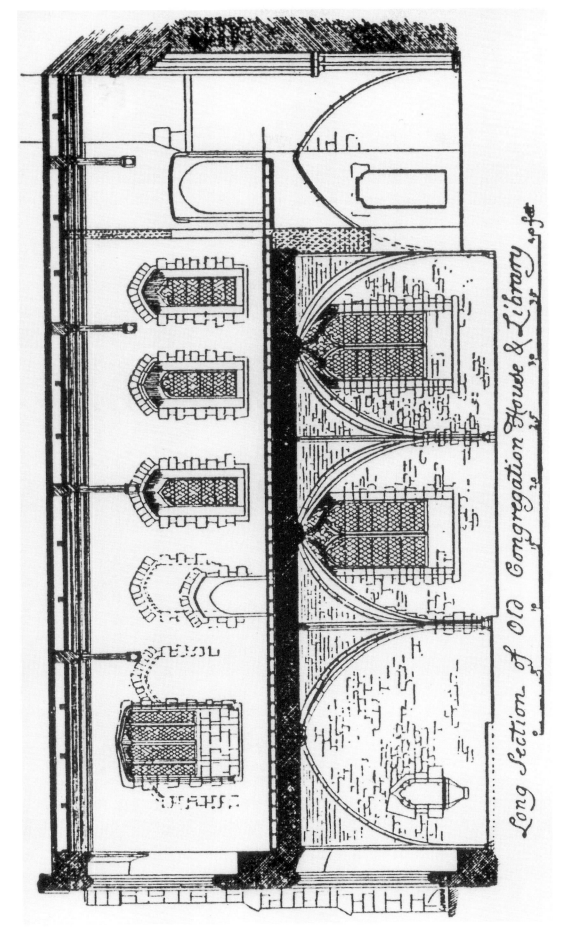

Long Section of Old Congregation House & Library

3   Merton College, south side of Mob Quad, 1371-78. Note single-light (16 inches wide) first-floor library windows with five and a half feet centres between. The larger, slightly later, gable-end window lights the central area between the two wings. The chapel tower (1451) is in the background. Today the general college library also occupies the former residential accommodation on the ground floor.

4   Divinity School and, above, Duke Humfrey's Library. 1420-88. A drawing made by John Bereblock which features in a volume illustrating Oxford buildings, presented to Queen Elizabeth in 1566 (MS Bodley 13, fol.16v). The view is from the north and shows a crenellated wall (not to be confused with the city wall – see plate 8) in the foreground. The entrance was at the west end and by means of stairs in the turrets on either side. Note the double-light windows in the library and the massive weighting pinnacles.

The verse text, translated into prose, reads: "The school which was built at your expense, Duke Humfrey, stands out and overlooks the rooftops at the centre of the city. It rises very high, its pinnacles are the tallest of all, a four-square building adorned with beautiful stone. Its noble ceilings gleam in the light from its many windows, and the stonework hanging there is bright with craftsman's handiwork. Founded in the reign of Henry VI by Humfrey, Duke of Gloucester, A.D. 1447". (Translation by Dr. Barker-Benfield).

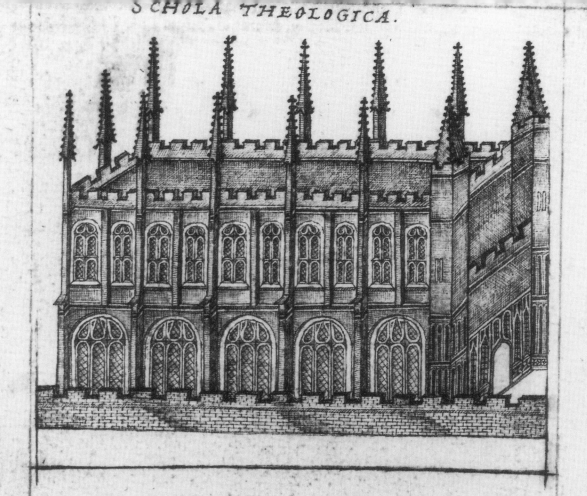

Cancell.

Eminet, & mediæ fastigia suspicit vrbis,
    Dux Humfrede, tuis sumptibus ista schola.
Surgit in immensum turritis vndiq pinnis.
    Sertaq perpulchro marmore, quadra domus.
Splendida luminibus crebris laquearia fulgent,
    Artificumq nitent pendula saxa manu.

Cœpit sub Henrico. 6º per dominū Humfredum.
Ducem Glocestriæ. Anno domini.   1441.

5   Cartouche at the foot of Sir Thomas Bodley's memorial by Nicholas Stone (after 1613) in Merton College chapel. The reclining figure represents Grammar and, holding a key, she gazes at the staircase shown on the left, said to depict one of those at the west end of the Divinity School leading up to Duke Humfrey's Library. The books on the right are by the grammarians Donatus, Diomedes and Priscian. For the whole monument see plate 16.

6   Duke Humfrey's Library, north wall during the restorations of the 1960s. Sir Thomas Bodley's large cases having been removed, the outline of one of the late fifteenth-century lecterns was revealed. Above its sloping shadow can also be seen the outline of the 1600 stalls and the black holes where their ties were inserted into the wall. Similar shadows have been found at New College. The works also showed how the insertion of the vaulting into the Divinity School caused the floor level of the library to come uncomfortably high under the window sills.

7   Drawing by Robert Potter, the architect of the Bodleian restorations, based on the lectern outlines and showing how the library must have looked in the early sixteenth century. The lecterns, without benches and with only one horizontal storage shelf, stand at right angles to the walls and hold chained volumes. The roof is supported by only six main trusses. The ceiling is boarded but has as yet no decorated panels. The end window would have faced east since no such equivalent is shown for the west end on Bereblock's drawing. This would therefore have been the view on entering from the turret stairs.

8   Ralph Agas's map of Oxford, made in 1578 and engraved in 1588, from the 1728 facsimile. The view is from the north and shows first the city wall and then the battlemented wall next to the Divinity School, the latter incorrectly shown as having four window bays. The Divinity School yard occupies what is now the garden of Exeter College. To the left lie the old University Schools, soon to be replaced, and their yard from which an ornamental gate leads past Brasenose College to the University Church of St Mary's, with, beyond it, St Mary's Hall, now Oriel College. To the left of the Schools is Catte Street where stationers and bookbinders traded. Also in view are New College, Hart Hall (now Hertford), All Souls and Lincoln Colleges. The number of trees indicates how open and rural even the city centre still was.

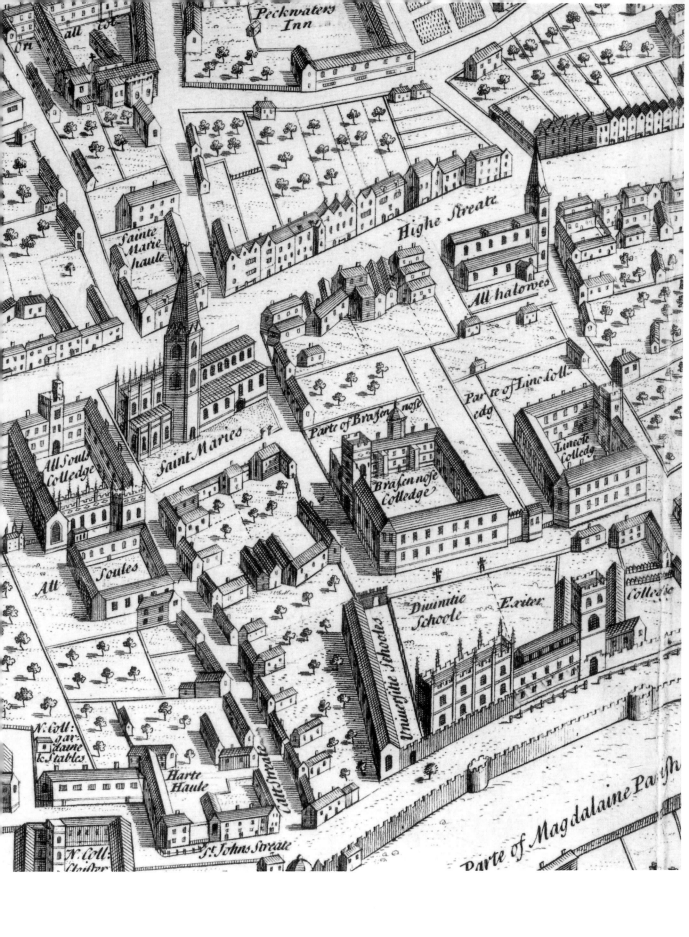

9   Part of David Loggan's 1675 view of Oxford showing the same area a hundred years after Agas. The Divinity School accurately has five window bays. In the foreground Wren's Sheldonian Theatre (1663-69) now straddles the line of the city wall although the private houses next to it still occupy the site of the future Clarendon Building (1711-15). The Divinity School and Duke Humfrey's Library have been enlarged by the addition of Arts End (1610) and the Schools quadrangle (1620) to the left and by that of Selden End (1640) to the right. The gate from the Old Schools yard is shown more clearly, as are the Catte Street houses, soon to give way to the Radcliffe Camera and its Square, while, to the left the old All Souls north quadrangle was to be re-developed with the Codrington Library balancing the chapel, visible here on the south side.

10   Merton Library, view from the central stairs (1760) looking north up the west range: room 1370s, roof 1503, furnishings 1589-90; decorative Jacobean panelling and plaster work c. 1620 with painted arms. The room beyond was originally that of the Sub-Warden, who also looked after the library, an arrangement found elsewhere. The central corridor is paved with medieval tiles [two thousand cost £7], here mostly covered with matting. The stall bookcases stand out between the window lights and are mortised into central end-beams running the length of the room. They have moulded cornices, and fluted semicircular pediments with plain vases at the ends. A framed 'table' indicates the subject shelved in the bay. Level, solid, desks rest on arm supports on either side of the stalls. The three shelves above originally contained chained books (some cases rearranged later to four shelves); the two below were added later. The fixed single-seat benches have moulded edges and plain ends.

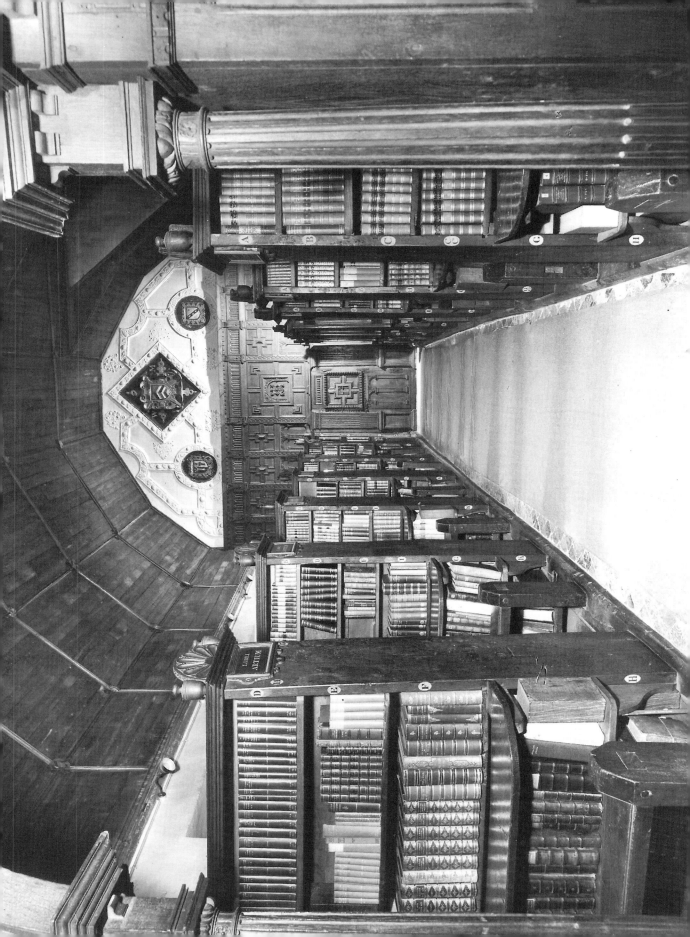

11   Merton Library, view into bay on the west side of the west wing, showing single-light window (16 inches) in splayed bay (41 inches). The reading desk (removed from the far bay) is solid and not hinged but shows the chain-gap. The filled-in remains of the original lower chaining bar can be seen in the middle of the shelf-end just below the desk level. The shelving and books below are a later addition. Note the rudimentary original bench morticed into the beams. The Jacobean panelling on the end-wall concealed the Sub-Warden's room.

12   Merton Library, south wing looking east. The entrance to this wing has an oak screen with Doric side columns, arcaded panels, entablatures, pediments and ball-finials. This wing was refitted in 1623 to match the west side. The fine end window, probably added at that time, lights a raised work area with grilled cupboards for rare items. The globe was a typical piece of older library furniture. The bench ends are more ornate. The stall ends show that Theology retained the favoured south-facing side. The oval shelf numbers are relatively modern. The left-hand case again shows the original two shelves, rearranged on most other stalls to take four.

13   Mob Quad, Merton College, west side, showing first-floor library windows and, in the roof area, the dormer windows of 1623. These were evidently added on both quad sides of the library in order to increase the light inside; but they were not repeated on the other, outer- and south- and west- facing sides. The ground-floor windows have largely been remodelled. The arch on the right leads through to the chapel, the Sub-Warden's room being above.

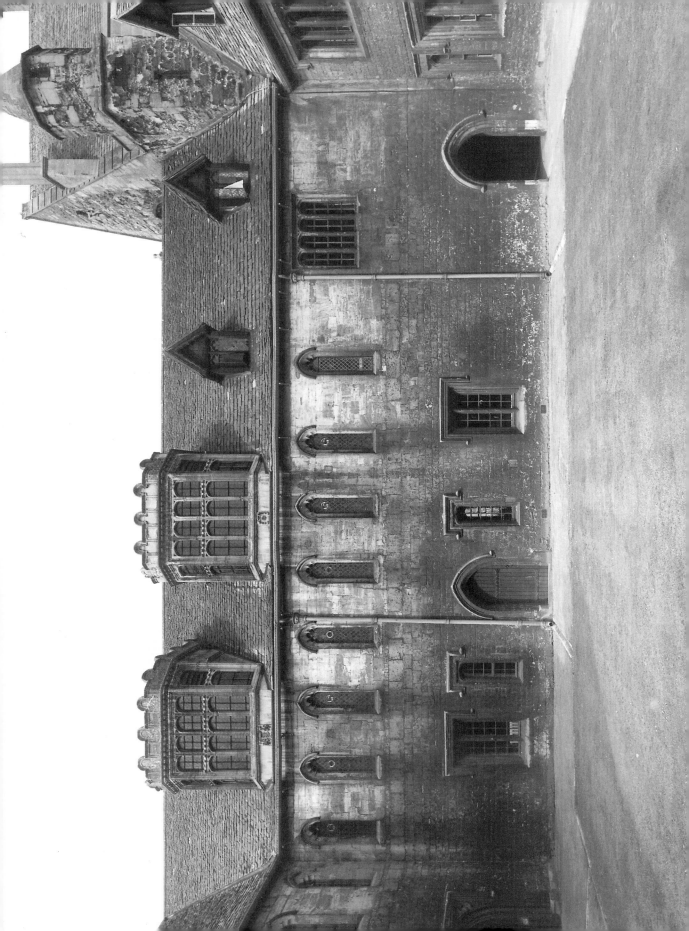

14   St John's College, Old Library, 1598. The first Oxford library designed specifically for stalls rather than lecterns, the bays are based on two-light windows and the room has a fine east-facing oriel window. Much stone and timber was economically obtained from the buildings of the former Carmelite friary on the western outskirts of the city, which belonged to the college. The barrel-vaulted ceiling is plastered and the central corridor is boarded. The generous bays (6 feet 3 inches) house archaic-looking benches at least some of which appear to have come from the former front quad lectern library, which had been refurnished as recently as 1584. The cases facing onto the central corridor are a modern addition, now removed. The bays nearest the door probably originally contained grilled cupboards for rare items. The stalls have been raised at some time by 18 inches and would at first have held only the three traditional shelves of chained books. The chains hung down into the still surviving chain-gap in the desks, which are here on a slight slope.

15   All Souls College, Old Library. Building before 1442. Lit by sixteen close-set windows, the library originally held lecterns calculated as being able to hold some 500 volumes. The room was remodelled in 1598, stalls being substituted for the lecterns. The magnificent plaster barrel-vault dates from the same period. When the Codrington Library came into use in 1750 the Old Library was partitioned to make a set for one of the Fellows, but the Elizabethan outer end-faces of the stalls were fortunately retained to form part of the wall panelling.

16   Merton College Chapel, alabaster and black marble monument to Sir Thomas Bodley, after 1613, supplied by Nicholas Stone at a cost of £200. Originally placed on the north wall immediately to the left of the altar, the monument was moved in the nineteenth century to the ante-chapel. Sir Thomas's bust is surrounded by four allegorical figures representing Music, Arithmetic, Rhetoric and Dialectic, all within pilasters of clasped books, fore-edge out. Above are the recumbant figures of Geometry and Astronomy, accompanied by geometrically shaped spheres [A 'mathematical pillar' with similar Platonic or Pythagorean solids and also resting on a pillar of books was presented to the Bodleian in 1620 and is now in the Museum of the History of Science]. Together with Grammar in the cartouche below, these figures make up the seven liberal arts. The figure at the top of the monument is Athena, just above Bodley's arms. On either side two further figures (Plenty and Charity in an original draft sketch) carrying, on the left, a book with the inscription 'Non delebo nomen eius de libro vitae' (Revelations 3.5) and on the right a crown (a Talmudic reference to Bodley's motto – see note to plate 24) thus representing both the Christian and Hebraic traditions. A contemporary reference suggests that since the only book not in the Bodleian was the Book of Life, Sir Thomas had gone to heaven to get it!

MEMORIÆ
THOMÆ BODLEY MERITIS PVBLICA
BIBLIOTHECA

17   Bodleian Library, Duke Humfrey's Library, looking west. Building 1480, furniture 1600. The size of the room (86 x 32 feet), far larger than any other Oxford library to date, is due to the layout of the Divinity School below. The fifteenth-century roof is finished with seventeenth-century painted panels bearing the arms of the University and, on the intersections, those of Bodley. The original, decorated, trusses with tie-beams alternate with later ones lacking them. The original three-shelf stalls (with no books under) have traces of the chaining hardware, of which only one specimen, partially reconstructed, survives. There are catalogue 'Tables' at the ends of the stalls. The original benches were replaced by chairs in 1756. The placing of the grille doors on the right is modern. Until c.1640 entrance would have been from the far end. By 1605 a gallery had had to be constructed over the far-end wall in order to accommodate small-format books and around 1693 further, longitudinal, galleries were added along the north and south walls, above the stalls and between the trusses. These were removed in 1877 and replaced by the portraits shown here. The wall structure had not been calculated to take the extra weight that the stalls and galleries imposed on it and in 1702 Sir Christopher Wren added buttresses on the south side. These were removed as part of the 1960s restoration and strengthening. The south-facing bays, on the left, were again reserved for Theology.

18   Duke Humfrey's Library, southern bays. Showing gilt subject guides and catalogue 'Tables'. Note that the insertion of the vauling into the Divinity School below raised the floor level producing very low window-sills. The original benches would have been lined up on the centre of the large two-light windows. The hinged desks were initially in one piece and could be held up by hooks let into the uprights of the stalls at either end. These desks were later divided to make three more manageable sections.

[Facing page]

19 Arts End, Bodleian Library, facing north, 1610. This first extension of the library was, when constructed, at the far end of the library and at the furthest point from the entrance, since, in the view of the day, the Arts were the least important subject. Here the growing number of Arts books and others in the smaller formats were shelved on the newer shelving system which placed them on shelves going round the walls. There were still three rows of chained books, used at desks as before and with benches in front of them, but a fourth row above (seen here immediately under the gallery) housed quartos behind grilled doors (long since removed but of which traces remain). The smaller formats were kept, in the newer Duke Humfrey's Library manner, on shelves in the gallery above, access to which could be restricted since it was by staircases, four of which were placed around the central area at the junction of the two rooms and in front of the east window. The volumes shown on the lower shelves here all have their spines facing outward in the post-1800 manner but a number of those in the gallery are still fore-edge out (for which, since they were never chained, there was no reason other than that was then the accepted system).

Central heating was first introduced into the Bodleian in 1845.

[Double page illustration overleaf]

20 Views of Arts End and of Selden End, the balancing extension at the west end of Duke Humfrey's Library, completed in 1640, both engraved by David Loggan in 1675. The upper one shows the Arts End system with its staircases and its grilled cupboards above the folio shelving. In the centre is Duke Humfrey's Library, starting with its grilled cupboards for rarer items and, on the right-hand wall, the bust of Charles I, presented in 1636. Bodley's bust, given in 1605, can just be seen in its original position on the left-hand (south) wall of Duke Humfrey. Note also the globes, then standard library furniture. By 1675, as now, entrance to the library was by means of the staircase coming up on the left. The engraving is correct in showing a member of the University in full academical dress (which was required by Statute) but incorrect in depicting visitors wearing swords, which were forbidden.

The sophistication of the Jacobean woodwork in Selden End (lower picture) marks the evolution of styles in the thirty years involved. However, the same shelving system was used, although here access to the galleries was by staircases hidden in the pedimented cupboards just visible at the beginning of Duke Humfrey's Library and then, having reached the gallery level, by passing under the central arch.

BIBLIOTHECÆ. BODLEIANÆ OXONIÆ. *Prospectus interior ab Oriente*

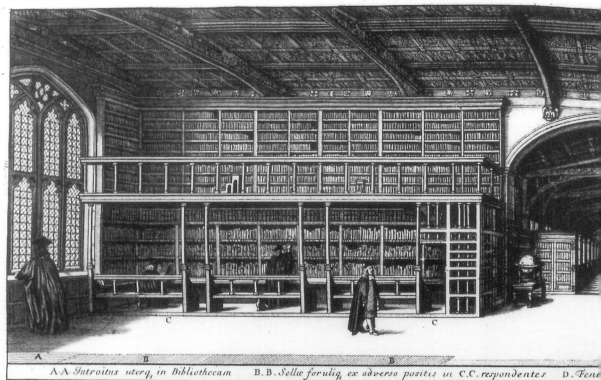

A.A. *Introitus uterq, in Bibliothecam*   B.B. *Sellæ foruliq, ex adverso positis in* C.C. *respondentes*   D. *Fene*

BIBLIOTHECÆ. BODLEIANÆ OXONIÆ. *Prospectus interior ab Occidente*

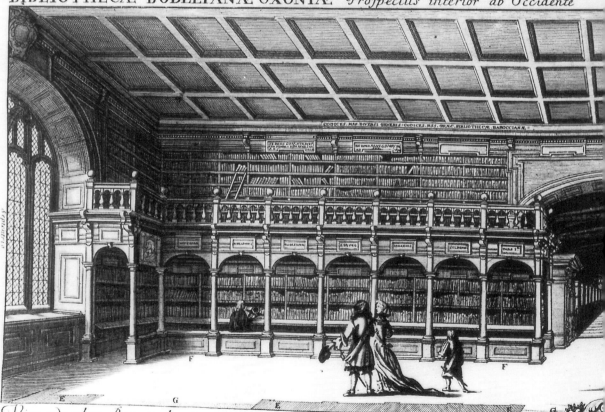

Viro admodum Reverendo vitæ integritate morum candore, spectatissimo; Scientiarum Academiæ ornamento; pro D.na *Margareta Comitissa Richmondiæ Theologiæ Professori V.N.E. Typum, Cui dum IPSE præfuit AVCTARIVM SELDENI Pelion sc. Ossæ gigan*

Dav. Loggan delin. et.

THE Inside of ẏᵉ Public or BODLEIAN LIBRARY in OXFORD from ẏᵉ East

Orientem.   E.E.Sellæ foruliq́ ex adverso positis in F F respondentes   G.G.G.Fenestræ ad Occidentem

THE Inside of ẏᵉ Public or BODLEIAN LIBRARY in OXFORD from ẏᵉ West

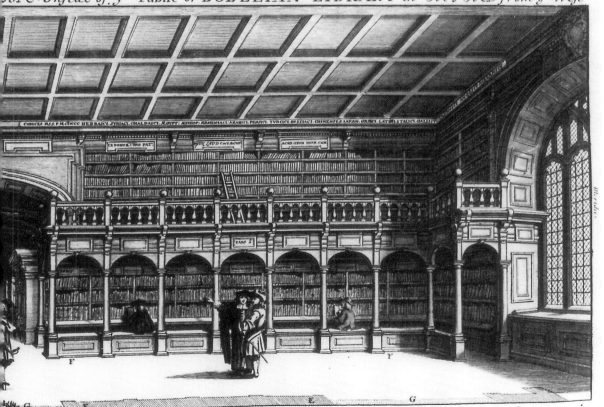

Insuper omnium Atlanti Dⁿᵒ THOMÆ BARLOVIO S.T. Dʳⁱ Collegÿ Reginensis Præposito,
ἀναντιρρήτω; et exteris hic hospitantibus semper Patrono Hunc BIBLIOTHECÆ BODLEI
teo nisu, sed felici conjecit; optimo jure, debitâq́ observantiâ   D.D.C.Q. Dav. Loggan

Sculp. cum Privil. S.R.M.

21   Bodleian Library, Schools Quadrangle, east face of the west range (1612). The Gothic window of Duke Humfrey, brought forward with the construction of Arts End, dominates this wall with its delicately ribbed panels. The rest of the quad (1620), with its large windows and vertical tracery, was left plain although the ribbed panelling was made to cover the corner staircases which gave access to the Schools lecture rooms and to the top floor gallery, intended for future book-storage space. The pinnacles, placed over the Divinity School/Duke Humfrey block for structural reasons, were continued around the quad and add greatly to the decorative effect.

The entrance to the library was through a staircase, here out of sight on the left but similar to that visible on the right. The central doorway led to the Proscholium or anteroom to the Divinity School. Since 1968 this has been the main entrance to the library. The bronze statue in front represents William Herbert, 3rd Earl of Pembroke, an early benefactor, and was made by Le Sueur in 1630.

22   Bodleian Library, Schools Quadrangle, west face of the east range, 1620. This shows the Tower of the Five Orders of Architecture (each level has columns in a different style) and, below, the Great Gate on to Catte Street. The statue is of King James I giving his works to Fame (on the left with trumpet) and to the University (kneeling humbly on the right). The volume actually presented in 1605 is still in the Library today. A tower was a common feature of many colleges (note in particular that at Merton), frequently occurring over the main gate. It was deemed a safe place and frequently held the archives; the University archives, strictly speaking separate from the Bodleian, have long been based in the tower. At various stages it has been suggested that the quadrangle should be either roofed over in glass or excavated to provide more storage space.

23   The Upper Reading Room, Bodleian Library. Constructed above the University's 'Schools', or lecture rooms, on the ground and first floors and completed in 1620, this was intended as future storage space but used initially as a picture gallery. The present layout dates from the reconstruction in the 1950s and caters for researchers in English literature and History. The ceiling initially had decorated panels but these were removed in the 1830s. The original frieze was then covered over but has been revealed by the recent works. The room extends round three sides of the quadrangle and seats some 200 readers.

24   A portion of the Upper Reading Room frieze arranged by the first Librarian, Thomas James, to give visitors to the picture gallery a panorama of writers chosen from among those whose works already reposed on the shelves of the Library. The frieze is some 230 metres in length and contains 200 portraits together with inscriptions and allegorical objects. It was based in part on A. Thevet, *Pourtraits et vies des hommes illustres* (1584). The north range covers the Arts, starting with Homer and ending with Sir Philip Sidney, the east range covers Medicine and Law, while on the south range, where the visitor entered, Theology demonstrated James's thesis that from the sub-Apostolic church through the Middle Ages and Reformation up to Jacobean England there had been a continuity of written witness against the pretensions of the Roman Church. This portion of the frieze, in the Tower Room, shows the two famous doctors, Galen (c. 129-99) and Avicenna (980-1037), together with a scroll bearing the library motto, 'Quarta perennis' (short for 'Quarta corona perennis erit', a Talmudic reference suggesting that beyond the three crowns of learning, priesthood and kingship, there was a fourth and greater one, that of a 'Good Name'). Some of the old roof panels can be seen above while a partially visible inscription below records William Laud's 1636 gift of his coin collection (now in the Ashmolean Museum), the foundation of one of the most comprehensive in England and another item then thought essential for a major university library.

25   Selden End, facing north. Completed in 1640, just before the Civil War, this extra accommodation immediately adjacent to Duke Humfrey's Library (to the right here), helped to cope with the enormous number of gifts coming in at the time, including Archbishop Laud's collection of manuscripts. The eventual donation of the library (some 8,000 volumes) of John Selden (1584-1654), a remarkably learned lawyer, increased the library by about fifty per cent and his collections were placed in the new accommodation, to which his name was then given. Selden's library was one of the largest put together in seventeenth-century England and was remarkable for its Western and Oriental manuscripts as well as for its outstanding accumulation, partly by gift, partly by purchase, of learned books.

26   David Loggan's general view from the south of the old Bodleian buildings, from his *Oxonia illustrata* of 1675, shows the whole of the library complex in the late seventeenth century. It emphasises the large leaded roof area, used on occasion such as for the drying of Thomas Tanner's books which had arrived wet after falling off a barge into the Thames. A sundial can also be seen to the left of the south face of the Upper Reading Room.

27   St John's College, the Canterbury Quadrangle. Archbishop Laud, earlier (1611–21) President of St John's, built this between 1631 and 1636. Open arcades on the east and west sides have central gateways with imposing Baroque frontispieces. That on the east side runs under the Laudian extension (at right angles) to the Old Library, which was conceived of more as a museum and locked storage area than as a reading room. The decorations to the arches, executed by the master mason, John Jackson, represent the Virtues on the west side and on the east, under the library, the Liberal Arts – Astronomy, Geometry, Music, Arithmetic, Logic, Rhetoric and Grammar plus Learning to fill the last space. All are shown together with appropriate instruments and books bearing the names of relevant classical authors on them. Geometry, on the right, is shown wearing a mural crown symbolizing Architecture and is flanked by the tools of that craft. In contrast to the Bodleian's Counter-Reformation frieze, Laud's return to an earlier iconographical tradition can be seen as part of his sustained attempt to restore something of the medieval system of thought.

28   Jesus College Library. The college was founded in 1571 and a first library was built in the 1630s but, probably for safety reasons, the building was demolished and the cases stored. A new library was completed in 1679. It presents an interesting evolutionary stage: the old cases for chained volumes, complete with their strapwork decoration, and the earlier openwork cresting over the entrance were re-installed but a wall-gallery was added above with later openwork panels. The library lies on a north/ south axis and was well lit by one large south window and numerous west-facing ones set high up in the wall. Despite the provision of the gallery it can also be seen very clearly that the number of smaller format books to be catered for has increased greatly and the shelving levels of the old chained folio days has had to be radically altered. The entablatures, fixed bench ends and other details are all of notable richness, although the flat ceiling with its wooden cornice is otherwise plain.

29   The Old Library, University College, 1672. Reputedly the oldest Oxford college and founded in 1249, University College had a library from 1391 but little accumulated there over the years. A new library was built over the kitchen (as at Wadham) in 1668-70 and a sketch of this survives in the college's Benefactors' book of 1674. The stall system is still the dominant feature but galleries run the length of the walls above. The ceiling is close-boarded and fine carved gates give access to the main area. For the later college library see plate 48.

30   The Old Library, St Edmund Hall. Building 1684. Unusually the library is located above the lobby to the chapel, a fact alluded to humorously by the pediment to the doorway to the latter being supported on piles of books. The library itself, shown here from an old photograph (c.1900), follows the new Arts End system of wall–shelves and gallery. The transverse cases at the ends of the stalls under the gallery are not original. The stickback Windsor chairs are similar to that of Oliver Goldsmith (d. 1774), now in the Victoria and Albert Museum. Note the large inkwell on the table, the continuing presence of the globe, the shields with benefactors' arms, and the lowerable electric light.

31   The Library, The Queen's College, north quad. This is as usual on the first floor but here in a free-standing classical building erected in 1695. It is eleven bays long and was originally open to the quad on the ground floor. The library was part of the very conscious general redevelopment of the college in the period 1670–1730 but was particularly stimulated by the bequest (in part, other books went to the Bodleian) of the collection of Bishop Barlow (d.1691). The design, sometimes attributed to Wren and formerly thought to be by Dean Aldrich, is clearly influenced by Wren's library at Trinity College, Cambridge, built 1676 to 1695. The ground floor open loggia was enclosed and converted to library use on receipt of a large benefaction in 1840. The main first-floor room is one of the most magnificent in Oxford, lying on a north/south axis and should be entered by the original south door (seen here at the far end). The library is still furnished on the stall system with hinged desks but pronounced entablature, the richness of the panels and of the carving of the remaining desk supports (some were removed in the nineteenth century) and the general spaciousness create a remarkable effect. The openwork cupboard doors (out of sight at the far end), in the style of Grinling Gibbons, are probably by Thomas Minn. The magnificent flat plaster ceiling is in three sections and may originally have been intended to contain paintings. The outer work dates from 1695 and is by James Hands while the later, inner, decoration (c.1756) is by Thomas Roberts. The height of the shelves has again been altered on many stalls and the 5,717 quartos and folios were unchained in 1780. From 1625 until 1840 senior undergraduates had a separate library – which was an unusal arrangement – but until 1938 the main library was reserved for Fellows and select M.A.s.

32   Christ Church. Completing the fourth (south) side of Peckwater Quad (built 1705-14 to the plans of Henry Aldrich, Dean of Christ Church), the library was designed by Dr George Clarke and started in 1717 but only finished in 1772. It replaced the earlier library previously installed in the old refectory of the former priory on the college site. The giant Corinthian columns start at ground level and support a monumental cornice with balustrade, the facade contrasting buff and white stone. It was originally intended to have an open ground floor but this was closed in around 1770 in order to create space to house a recent gift of pictures (now converted to library use).

33   Christ Church, the Library, first floor. The library proper is on the first floor and has seven large north-facing windows and Venetian type ones on the east and west. It has wall-shelving to the south with a gallery above and offices behind. There is further wall-shelving on the north wall between the windows, some tiers having two frontispieces. Above the cases is ornate plaster work by Thomas Roberts and, beyond, divided into three panels, further plaster work, the larger middle panel being coved. The stools, made by Thomas Chippendale in 1764, were for use at the two large baise-covered tables. Note too the braziers, the only form of heating. Until the early nineteenth century the library was reserved for senior members and noblemen.

34   The Codrington Library, All Souls College, south face of the north range of the north quad. Hawksmoor developed the whole quadrangle, basing himself on the south side fifteenth-century chapel which he retained. Since the chapel and hall filled the south side, the library had to balance them on the north, thus dictating both its size, exterior style, and its groundfloor placement. Work on the library started in 1716 and was completed in 1750. The large central sundial was designed by Christopher Wren in 1658/9 (he was a Fellow and bursar of the college in that year), and was moved to the library from its original position over the south front of the chapel in 1877.

35   The Codrington Library, interior. If the exterior is Gothic, the interior of the library is in contrast totally Palladian with Venetian-style end-windows. As a result of its planning imperatives it is the longest library room in Oxford, being roughly two hundred feet by thirty feet by forty feet high. The shelving is in grilled cases on floor level and on an open gallery above. It is adjustable having hole and peg fixtures which are among the earliest in Oxford. Hawksmoor had proposed a second gallery but did not proceed with it. The upper cornice carries alternating urns and busts of former Fellows. At both levels the high shelves require steps, although the large ones on ground floor are a relatively recent acquisition. Some of the chairs and individual free-standing desks may be original. The statue of Christopher Codrington, on the left, is by Henry Cheere (1734), that at the end is of Sir William Blackstone, the jurist, and is by John Bacon (1784). The lunch at Encaenia (the major annual honorary degree ceremony) is traditionally held here. Certain Fellows are also recorded as having played cricket here (with a tennis ball) in 1924.

36   A proposal for the Radcliffe Camera, 1712. Dr John Radcliffe (1652-1714), a successful London doctor, proposed, before his death, to fund an extension to the Bodleian. Various sites contiguous with the Bodleian buildings were put forward, as were alternative shapes: some of these being rectangular ones which would have filled most of the area between St Mary's and the Schools quadrangle. The latter provided a number of study rooms and considerable book storage space as can be seen from this plan, which may have been influenced by Wren's library for Trinity College, Cambridge. In this proposal high wall-shelving (including a gallery) only allows the light to come in from the semi-circular top lights. An extensive basement provided further storage and space. From a library point of view therefore this was among the best proposals made in early eighteenth-century Oxford. It became clear however that Radcliffe had sought something monumental at all costs and eventually the authorities settled for a round free-standing building (Wren had suggested an oval shape for Trinity in 1676) which would replace the poorer Catte Street houses. Hawksmoor, whose Clarendon Building was completed in 1715 and who was engaged at All Souls, made numerous designs and combined them with his aim of opening up the medieval street plan with some town planning on a grander basis, thus giving Oxford alternative 'city' and 'university' centres, the latter largely centred on the Bodleian. This town-planning came to nothing. (Ashmolean Museum, Gibbs I -125).

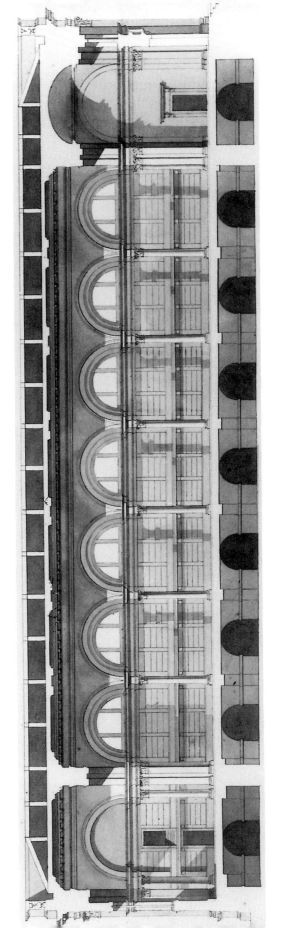

37   The Radcliffe Camera, northern elevation, viewed from the steps of the Bodleian. Radcliffe's benefaction only became available in 1736 but the concept of a rotunda had already been established by Hawksmoor, who died in that year. James Gibbs took over the project which was completed in 1749. Eight large arched and pedimented bays formed the ground floor and allowed for open access to the central area from whence a fine internal staircase went up to the library on the first floor. Coupled Corinthian columns then support an imposing cornice and balustrade with balls, eventually leading to the drum and charcteristic dome. In 1863 the ground floor archways were closed with windows and the flight of stairs opposite the Bodleian was added when the library became a student reading room for the University. The surrounding grass area was enclosed with metal railings in 1827. These were were removed in 1935, and restored in 1993. In 1912 a large storage area was created for the Bodleian under the paving and grass between the two buildings and was filled with rolling metal bookcases.

38   The Radcliffe Camera, Main Reading Room, first floor. View from the entrance. A magnificent room, the eight stone piers having a gallery at mid-height and arches above with excellent cartouches in the spandrels. There are garlands between the windows and a dome with painted hexagonal coffering. The plasterers employed were the best in England. The original floor is in black and white marble but was covered with matting in the nineteenth century when students' boots made too much noise. Note the wall bookcases, all fitted with wire-meshed fronts and having adjustable, slotted, shelving – an early example. The window-side desks are wide and sloping. Book shelving is however not generous and as Pevsner puts it 'no library is more of a monument and more liberal with space'. The room has twice served for grand dinners; once in 1814, and again in 1986 when the Prince of Wales dined in connection with the fund-raising Campaign for Oxford.

This eighteenth-century view comes from J. Gibbs, *Bibliotheca Radcliviana*, London 1747, plate XIV.

39   Worcester College Library, 1736. Built on the first floor as part of the main early eighteenth-century development, the library is over the cloister and west facing. Open meshed cupboards house books on shelves which are slotted (and therefore adjustable) on the central cupboard tiers and fixed on the side tiers. This may be the earliest Oxford example of the adjustable shelf. There is a gallery with an ornate iron railing going round three sides of the room. The setting sun has evidently caused considerable damage to the west-facing leather-bound books. The columns and general decoration look surprisingly late eighteenth-century and neo-classical. The general design, and possibly the detailed subject grouping of the books on their adjustable shelves, are usually attributed to Dr George Clarke, benefactor, who died in 1736.

40   Brasenose College Library. The first floor library, which dates from 1664, is above the former cloister. It was restored by James Wyatt in 1780. Once again this change was prompted by the bequest of a large number of books, in this case those of Principal Francis Yarborough (died 1770). Wyatt blocked the west windows with book shelves and inserted a vaulted plaster ceiling of segmented panels with restrained decoration. This early Wyatt restoration is still in the neo-classical style and contrasts with his later Gothicising work. There were no protruding tables or shelves and since in the nineteenth century undergraduates were not admitted the Fellows played badminton in the library, their 1879 rackets being preserved there. In 1894 the library was reorganised and the stall-type shelving shown here inserted. The stall cases have a separate lower section for larger books and are raised on their own turned feet. The south end is apsed, has locked cupboards for rarer material, and served in the traditional manner as a reading area for the Fellows while elsewhere storage clearly had priority, a natural attitude since undergraduate use of the library was only allowed in 1897. It is noticeable that the only floor-covering is that in the central area. The shelving was painted white and the ceiling picked out in colour as part of a further restoration in the 1950s. The bust in the foreground is that of Richard Grenville, 1st Duke of Chandos and Buckingham (1776-1839), who matriculated at Brasenose in 1791.

41   Oriel College Library, 1788. This beautiful free-standing Palladian library, on the first floor, is wedged in between two now visually important trees. The ground floor, containing common rooms, is rusticated while above plain Ionic columns support a simple cornice. The high wall-shelved interior with its south-facing windows has an unusual apse at one end with two giant scagliola columns. The construction of the library was prompted by a large bequest of books by Edward, fifth Baron Leigh (1742-86).

42   Balliol College Library, 1816. At Balliol the library proper occupies one of the technically oldest parts of the college in that the building was constructed between 1430 and 1490. It was however extensively remodelled by James Wyatt in 1792-94 in the, at that date new, reversion to the Gothic style. The library on the north side of the front quadrangle retains its eleven close-set, two-light windows but has added battlements. Inside the stall-type cases equally have Gothic tops designed by Wyatt and a plaster rib-vault. From an original watercolour by J. Malchair now at Balliol.

43   Bodleian Library, Arts End, looking south about 1843, after a watercolour by R.W. Buss (1804-75), now in the Bodleian. The Librarian, Dr Bulkeley Bandinel (or possibly a younger deputy), sits at his desk (made in 1832) looking down Duke Humfrey's Library and controlling the entrance which is to his left. He sits in the high-backed special chair (still in this position today) and made the previous year from oak removed from the Picture Gallery (Upper Reading Room). Everyone wears full academical dress including 'mortarboard' hat. A sloping exhibition case stands in the middle of the room and the portraits of former librarians hang from the gallery. The old stairs up to the latter have been removed and access is now by means of stairs in the study half hidden to the right and then through a hole (invisible from this angle) in the wall. A bridge has been added across the window on which an elderly academic is, somewhat surprisingly and indeed improbably, seated. The same stairs gave access to the galleries then running along the upper parts of the walls of Duke Humfrey's Library and the books on these shelves can just be seen. Below the bust of Sir Thomas Bodley is the fourteenth-century Gough map of England and, below that, the library catalogues. The person to the right is about to take the one step down from Duke Humfrey (not yet known under that name) into Arts End.

44   The Taylor Institution, 1848. Built, after competition, to the designs of C.R. Cockerell, the Institution, the University's centre for European languages, shares a complex with the Ashmolean Museum. The St. Giles' Street facade is striking with two high storeys, an attic floor and a notable projecting entablature. Four large Ionic columns project, framing the windows of the Main Reading Room, and carry female statues by W.G. Nicoll representing the literatures of Italy, France, Germany and Spain. The groundwork is in buff-coloured stone, the decorative parts in white. A frieze fills in at the attic level and basket-weave ornamentation surrounds the whole building.

Pevsner sees the front as powerful and perfectly integrated and better than the other sides of the complex. He suggests that the whole is an informed combination of classical forms, used intentionally but with different effects in various parts. The Taylorian and Ashmolean complex thus points the way from the classicism of the early nineteenth century to the baroque traits of the later decades.

The building, with an extension built by T.H. Hughes in the 1930s, houses library facilities as well as lecture rooms.

45   The Taylor Institution Library, Main Reading Room. This grand forty foot cube was conventional in having bay bookshelves, originally all protected by mesh grilles, and a gallery with cupboards and unprotected shelves. The lower woodwork is all in oak but the higher decorative elements are all oak-grained to a high standard. The library was unusual in that it had a large central fireplace with a fine bronze surround and the founder's portrait framed in marble. There is a high semi-domed ceiling. The large windows on both east and west fronts cause environmental problems. The floor has a two-colour inlaid hexagonal design in wood, which picks up the gallery and ceiling design, but this has had to be covered up by carpet. Much early furniture survives despite the necessary introduction of modern technology, such as the on-line catalogue terminals seem here in the fireplace just before the removal of the old card-catalogue in its stand on the right.

46   Proposed Venetian Gothic bridge to link the Upper Reading Room and the Radcliffe Camera, 1858. The increasing use of the Bodleian in the mid-nineteenth century led to the use of part of the old Picture gallery as a reading room and, in the eighteen-sixties, not only to the opening of the Radcliffe Camera for student use but also to the enclosure of its ground floor. The Radcliffe Librarian, Sir Henry Acland, thought that a link between these areas would be a great convenience and a first-floor corridor (with a 'double incline for book-trucks on rails'), as illustrated, was proposed. Like a number of other solutions to library problems at the time this was fortunately not adopted and an entrance and steps at ground floor level, coming into the existing internal staircase, were eventually inserted. Reproduced from the sketch by Benjamin Woodward, now in the Radcliffe Science Library.

47   The Oxford Union Society Library. Established for debating in 1823, the Union moved to St Michael's Street and built a debating hall in 1857. Designed by Benjamin Woodward in the Gothic style, it was decorated by Rossetti, Morris, Burne-Jones and others with scenes from the Morte d'Arthur (faded despite restoration), the ceiling being further decorated by Morris first with grotesque creatures and later in a lighter design. A new debating hall was built in 1878, the former one then becoming the library to which a new part was added in 1910. The new "Old Library" retains a wonderful period atmosphere, recalling traditional clubland. The two central fireplaces, back to back, have under-the-floor flues. The Union library was for long the main source of books for undergraduates.

48   University College Library. The old library (see plate 29) was replaced in 1861 by the present building by Sir George Gilbert Scott in the middle-pointed Gothic style. An undergraduates' library had existed since the late eighteenth century and the library, as shown here after an old postcard of around 1900, was designed for all members of the college. The high projecting bay shelving has the conventional nineteenth-century nine shelves which are moveable and allow for larger books on the two lower shelves. The centre aisle is carpeted and leads to two cold but imposing statues (10 tons of Carrara marble, 1847) of Lords Eldon and Stowell, former members of the college. An ironwork gallery gave access to further shelving at a higher level. Despite this, space had become a major problem by 1915 and the college, like others, deposited some of its books in the Bodleian. In 1937 however it was still found necessary to insert a mezzanine floor.

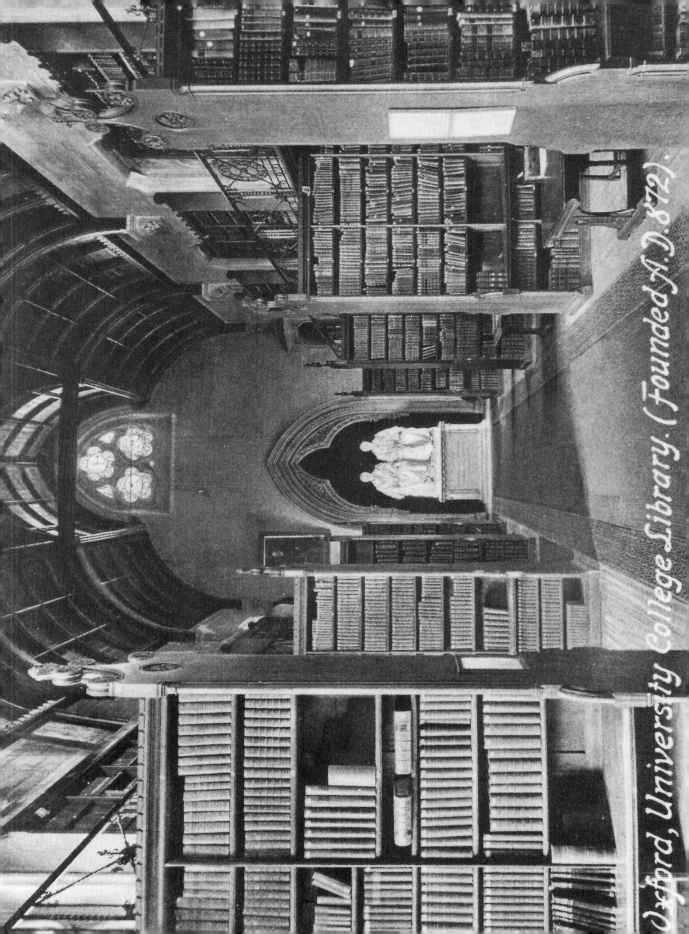

Oxford, University College Library. (Founded A.D. 872).

49   Balliol College, The Reading Room, after a postcard of *c.*1900. The former west range hall (built originally in the mid-fifteenth century) had large windows and, after the construction of the new hall, was converted to library use in the 1870s. It housed a separate library for undergraduates first instituted by the energetic and forward-looking Master, Benjamin Jowett. Here the wall cases have nine rows of shelves for standard octavo-sized books while larger volumes are on island cases. There is an open fire (with numerous books above) and the doorway is curtained. The lighting is by electricity although the central chandelier may well have been a gasolier. A ventilator appears to be provided high above the window. The table desks are flat although some sloped lecterns are available. A coin display, busts, and books laid out abound. Some cases appear to be behind closed grilles. The plaster casts on the wall represent, above, the Parthenon metopes and, below, its frieze. The portrait is that of Richard Prosser, a library benefactor. A mezzanine was inserted in 1960.

Oxford, Balliol College Library. (Founded 1263.)

50   Keble College Library. Built on the south side of the main quadrangle at the same time as the chapel on the north, the library is by William Butterfield and dates from 1878, being the gift of fervent Tractarians. The college and the library are, unusually for Oxford at that date, in brick with polychrome patterns and bands, the whole in High Victorian Gothic both externally and internally. The library (86 ft long) has a series of side bays, all of which had openwork gates and were for storage, the reading area being at the far end under Holman Hunt's well-known painting, 'The Light of the World' which originally hung there. Despite its height, the library has no gallery owing to the size of the windows.

51   Mansfield College Library, 1889. The college architect was Basil Champneys who continued to work in the Gothic style. The library is one of the best parts, having an impressive roof supported by tall timber posts and enlivened by floridly painted roof panels. The side bays resemble those at Keble but are not so shut in. Here there is also a low gallery. The cupboards have linen-fold panelling with consultation lecterns above.

52   The Public Library, the Town Hall, Oxford. Before 1893. Opened in 1854, four years after the Public Libraries Act, the Oxford Public Library was initially for reference only. The open loggia under the old Town Hall, built in 1751, was converted to house the library. The room shows every sign of being an adaptation. Numerous books are provided, piled high on one table, and, in a traditional manner, periodical parts are laid out at each seat. Chairs are simple, desks are wide and leather lined. The shelves have dust-trap leather edgings. Lighting is by gas and there is an open fire.

53   The New Town Hall, built in 1893-97 to the designs of Henry T. Hare, was ostentatiously Jacobean. The City Library, opened in February 1896, appears to have become more professional in that the reading area of this reference section is now separate from the bays of shelves (including those in the new gallery) and a formal counter can be seen halfway down on the right, flanked by two busts which appear to be different from those in the earlier illustration. The lighting is by electricity, no open fire is visible, and the desks, still with their periodicals, are sloping. The furniture, as the furnishings generally, are distinctly Jacobean. The windows are curtained and there are exhibition cases on the left. A large notice at the far end enjoins 'SILENCE'. The Lending Library, Newspaper Reading Room, and Ladies' Room were on the ground floor.

54   The Radcliffe Science Library. Following the taking over of the Radcliffe Camera as a Bodleian reading room, the Radcliffe scientific books were transferred to the new University Museum. In 1901 a new library, funded by the Drapers' Company, was built to the designs of Sir T.G. Jackson (wing to the right of the plate) but proved insufficient to house the growing literature of science. In 1927 the Radcliffe Library formally became a part of the Bodleian Library and was renamed the Radcliffe Science Library. As part of the reorganization of the Bodleian in the 1930s an extension (to the left) was added in 1934 by Sir Hubert Worthington. Some inscriptional work and certain inside doors were by Eric Gill (see Back Cover). See also illustration 69.

55   St Edmund Hall, Undergraduate library, 1921. For much of the late nineteenth century undergraduates had to make do with the Radcliffe Camera general reading room and with that of the Oxford Union Society (the debating centre). Progressively colleges began to make provision for their own students but, as can be seen here, this was often in the spartan style of the period. Note the bare boards, the rudimentary wooden furniture, the card catalogue on the left, and the borrowing register on the lectern desk. The adjustable shelving is supported by metal tags slotted into metal strips inserted into the uprights and sometimes called "Tonks" fittings.

56   Rhodes House and its library. Described by Pevsner as 'a curious wedding of high-roofed Cotswold and classical copper-domed rotunda', the building was put up in 1930 by Sir Herbert Baker. Built as a memorial to Cecil Rhodes, it serves as a centre for Commonwealth and American studies. Its library is a branch of the Bodleian and besides reading rooms (with much woodwork in the colonial style) it has another large underground storage area. A new centre for specifically American studies is planned.

57   St Hilda's College, the Library. The creation of libraries, provided for students rather than, as elsewhere, for the Fellows, was an early imperative in an Oxford which only accepted women as equals in 1920. St Hilda's (founded in 1893), starting from a restricted basis in connection with Cheltenham Ladies College, could initially only afford to convert existing houses. The red brick neo-Georgian Burrows Building, which includes the library, was only built in 1934 to the designs of Sir Edwin Cooper. Sited on the ground floor, it has accommodation above and had a storage basement (converted into a reading room in 1978) below. The interior is traditional with a good gallery and is divided into a series of bays which are cosy but somewhat dark. The plain oak panelling throughout is a distinctive feature.

58   St Hugh's College, the Library. Established in 1886 as a woman's college (which it remained until 1977), St Hugh's buildings are in neo-Georgian red brick and date from 1916. The women's colleges early established libraries in order to provide on-site for their students. This library building dates from 1936 and shows the typical pattern of the period: plain windows, top lighting and ventilation, largely devoid of decoration, strip lighting, and sound but unornamented furniture. There is Lino flooring; good, if plain, working desks are placed within the bays which have a maximum provision of six easily reachable shelves.

59   Campion Hall. The Society of Jesus established itself in Oxford in 1896 and completed its buildings, to the designs of Sir Edwin Lutyens, in 1936. The well-stocked library has commodious bays, curtains, a parquet floor, and armchairs (perhaps of the 1950s) rather than desks, indicating a more social use. It is redolent of comfortable ease and of some aspects of the inter-war years in Oxford, of Ronald Knox's *Let Dons Delight* (1939) and of *Brideshead Revisited* (1945).

60 The New Bodleian Library. By Sir Giles Gilbert Scott, built 1937–39. Apparently only three storeys high and recessed from the street, this stone building has minor exterior decoration which is dominated by a non-functional doorway (used only for the opening ceremony) which really serves as a focal point for the vista across the road from the Schools Quadrangle and through the centre of the Clarendon Building. An external ring of administrative rooms thus masks an eleven-storey pyramidal bookstack which has three levels below ground and houses some five million volumes. A U-shaped conveyor system carries boxes down the centre of the core, under the street through a tunnel, and up in the Old Library for delivery in the Upper Reading Room.

61   New Bodleian Library, bookstack. The pyramidal stack floors are supported by a steel frame. Most are entirely artificially lit and internal temperature and humidity are controlled. Shelving is slotted metal shelving of standard size. It is in free-standing islands since a measure of open access was expected. Only the recently shelved bottom floor has compact, rolling shelving. Orders are sent from reading rooms by pneumatic tube and the books returned in boxes on a conveyor-belt system.

62   The Plant Sciences Library. Started in 1905 as the School of Forestry and becoming in 1938 the Commonwealth Forestry Institute, this library has an international reputation. The building, by Worthington, dates from 1950. The rooms are generously designed, have cork-tile floors, overhead fitted lighting, and, of course, a generous use of wood which, as in the PPE (Philosophy, politics and economics) Reading Room in the New Bodleian, came designedly from many different parts of the British Commonwealth. The tables have padded seating of a traditional kind and table dividers.

63   Nuffield College. Founded by William Morris, Lord Nuffield, the local motor-car millionaire, in 1937 and established as a graduate college in social studies, the college buildings were only completed in 1960. They were designed by Harrison, Barnes & Hubbard in a Cotswold style inspired by Lutyens. A striking feature at the western (railway) entrance to Oxford and immediately opposite the Norman castle mound is the library tower which, with its three restricted windows per side on each floor, leads up to a tall spire. Thus book storage does not take up prime ground area and yet gives notable character to the college and indeed to the area.

64   The St Cross Building. Constructed in 1964 by Sir Leslie Martin and Colin St John Wilson, this houses three separate units: the Bodleian's Law Library, the Faculty of English, and the Institute of Economics and Statistics, each having their own library. The libraries are largely sited in the centre of the relevant wing while broad central steps give access. Typical of the University's *ad hoc* planning is the assembly of three relatively unconnected subjects in one building: they share lecture facilities but not common rooms or libraries. The original, rather stark but powerful, lines have been softened by the growth of the trees just to the right of this early picture.

65   The Law Library, St Cross Building. The Bodleian's Law Library houses one of the largest collections of legal literature outside the United States. With the Radcliffe Science Library and the Rhodes House Library, it is a separate establishment of part of the Bodleian stock. It contains close on half a million volumes and has some 300 seats. Most of its books are on open access and the library is also liberally provided with study carrels for the increasing number of graduate students in this field. The carrels are placed near the windows while the open stacks frame the main reading area in the centre. This has top natural lighting but otherwise its serried ranks of desks – in contrast with the earlier tradition of more individualized study now reserved only for graduates – and the tighter strip-lit desks betray the era of mass higher education.

66   The History Faculty Library, housed in the former Indian Institute. Built in 1885 in the English Palladian style by Basil Champneys, the Institute served to provide courses for the Indian Civil Service. In 1968 the library was moved to penthouse accommodation on top of the New Bodleian and the History Faculty Library, expanding like other faculty libraries at that date, moved into its modernized premises. The strong colours and careful lighting make the most of the elegant interior while the banks of strip-lit desks are characteristic of the period. History is one of the largest Arts faculties at Oxford and history students make heavy use both of this library, and of the adjacent Bodleian, and Codrington libraries.

67   The Central Library, Oxfordshire County Library Service. This successor to the old City Library (see illustrations 52 & 53) was constructed in the Westgate shopping centre in 1973 and opened by Her Majesty Queen Elizabeth the Queen Mother. It was built by the Oxford City Council before the 1974 local government reorganization created a single Oxfordshire County Library service. The first floor, shown here, houses an integrated lending and reference library. Spatially open and with easy seating it caters for a large readership who visit in order to select for home reading. Staff telephones are in evidence and computer-based or online catalogues are in use. Both shelving and furniture are moveable within the core of the building space which is treated more on the lines of a general commercial store. This library is used by many students in Oxford, some belonging to Oxford University but others being part of the city's large student population attending private educational establishments or language schools. Oxford Brookes University (formerly the Oxford Polytechnic) has its own considerable library facilities with which Oxford University co-operates in some fields. The University is also closely linked with library facilities for the National Health Service through the Cairns Library at the John Radcliffe Hospital.

68   All Saints Church, converted in the 1970s to form Lincoln College Library. The church was built in 1708, possibly to the designs of Henry Aldrich, Dean of Christ Church. Sometimes described as one of the most perfect English churches of its day, the exterior being notable for its spire and the interior having no aisle, chancel or apse, and a flat roof. Becoming redundant in the 1970s, it was converted into a library for the adjacent Lincoln College. The floor was raised in order to allow for use on two levels in a spacious and unobtrusive manner while retaining many original features. The architect of the restoration was Robert Potter with the Rector of the college at the time, Sir Walter Oakeshott, playing an active role. The costs of the expensive transformation (including unobtrusive double-glazing) were partly met by the Pilgrim Trust.

69   Radcliffe Science Library, Lankester Reading Room. For the first two stages of the RSL's modern building, see illustration 54. The great growth of Oxford science after the Second World War required further space which was provided in the 1970s by creating a large reading room under part of the lawn in front of the University Museum. The reading room, with its supporting pillars, was opened in 1975 and named after its architect, Jack Lankester, then University Surveyor. Here a careful choice of materials and clean lines attempt to produce 'psychological habitability' without decoration or exterior view – something like designing the interior of a luxury liner. The two levels cover in all half an acre and contain 13,000 feet of shelving for books in the physical sciences, together with 276 reader seats.

70   The University Book Repository, Nuneham Courtenay. Visually the most surprising and unlikely of Oxford libraries, this is tucked away in the vegetable garden of an eighteenth-century country house some eight miles out of Oxford. The Repository, the concept of which was first discussed in connection with plans for the New Bodleian in the 1930s but which was actually taken up and started in 1975, provides temperature and humidity controlled long-term storage for the University's libraries of permanent retention. Administered by the Bodleian, it has mobile, compact, shelving. The present five sections hold some 1.5 million volumes and there is planning permission for a further three sections. The growth of the University's collections for permanent retention, either through the legal deposit regulations (the Bodleian is the oldest of the six British deposit libraries) or by acquisition (from abroad) which comes to some 100,000 volumes, requires around three thousand linear metres of new shelving annually.

Copyright © Oxford Bibliographical Society 1995

Occasional Publication No. 25

THE OXFORD BIBLIOGRAPHICAL SOCIETY was founded in 1922 to encourage bibliographical research by holding meetings, by arranging visits to libraries, and by publishing monographs for distribution to members. Membership is open to all who are interested in the objects of the Society, subject to their being elected by the Council. Enquiries should be addressed to the Society, c/o The Bodleian Library, Oxford OX1 3BG.

Typeset in Bembo and printed in Great Britain at
The Alden Press, Oxford

71   The Nissan Centre for Japanese Studies was built in 1993 in the grounds of St Antony's College to the designs of the Architects Design Partnership. The Centre is a University establishment and houses within its library the Japanese Collections of the Bodleian, this part being a Dependent Library of the Bodleian. Although surrounded by Gothic Revival houses, a former convent, and collegiate architecture including a modern prize-winning concrete structure, it achieves a certain oriental style. At the date of writing it is Oxford's latest library although others are projected, some extensions, some replacements, some to cater, as here, for developing new studies.